D0731166

Ali Edwards

A DESIGNER'S eye

for scrapbooking

CREATING
Keepsakes
SCRAPBOOK MAGAZINE

BY BECKY HIGGINS

A Place For Everything

As you probably know, I've always enjoyed organizing my life and my home. My scrapbook room has specific "homes" for my paper, my ribbons, my pens. In fact, "a place for everything and everything in it's place," is one of my favorite organizational principles.

It's only natural to apply this same principle to my scrapbook pages, so I am especially excited to have this book as one of my new favorite resources. In *A Designer's Eye for Scrapbooking*, Ali Edwards teaches us how to think of a blank piece of cardstock as a foundation for a layout—and how to divide that foundation into individual "homes" for photographs, journaling and embellishments.

And that's just one of the many things I learned by looking through Ali's "designer's eye" on scrapbooking. I loved her ideas on creating balance and flow on my pages, as well as learning how to mix and match a variety of page elements in an eye-appealing fashion. I found the layouts in this book to be just like Ali herself—inspirational and charming! I think you'll find, as I did, that this book is an invaluable guide for creating well-designed scrapbook pages that will be treasured for many years.

Ali teaches us that there is "a place for everything." She's certainly found her place in the world of scrapbooking. As a graphic designer who also happens to be a talented scrap-booking artist, Ali brings a unique perspective to the world of scrapbook page design.

Enjoy discovering a place for your memories,

Becky Higgins

founding editor | Lisa Bearnson

co-founder | Don Lambson

editor-in-chief | Tracy White

special projects editor | Leslie Miller

senior writer | Rachel Thomae

copy editor | Kim Sandoval

editorial assistants | Joannie McBride, Fred Brewer

art director | Brian Tippetts

designer | Erin Bayless

production designers | Just Scan Me!

production director | Gary Whitehead

publisher | Mark Seastrand

vice president, group publisher | David O'Neil

SVP, group publishing director | Scott Wagner

VP, group CFO | Henry Donahue

PRIMEDIA Inc.

chairman | Dean Nelson

president & CEO | Kelly Conlin

vice-chairman | Beverly C. Chell

TRADEMARKS
Trademarked names are used throughout this book. Rather than put a trademark symbol in every occurrence of a trademarked name, we state we are using the names only in an editorial fashion and to the benefit of the trademark owner with no intention of infringement of the trademark.

www.creatingkeepsakes.com

Printed and bound in the U.S.A.
ISBN 1 929180 68 3

How to
USE THIS BOOK

This book is packed with ideas, information and inspiration. There are several different ways that you can use this book. Here are a few suggestions to get you started:

1. Flip through the book and study each layout for inspiration and ideas. Tag the pages you want to refer back to again with sticky notes.

2. Read the text and learn how to create well-designed pages from Ali's unique perspective. Make notes on how four other scrapbook designers (Tina, Mellette, Joy and Carrie) applied Ali's principles to their own pages. Then, challenge yourself to take the same "assignment" and apply the principles on your layouts.

3. Use this book as your personal "style guide." Do the exercises in chapters 6 and 7 and then read the book from front to back, marking layouts that appeal to your personal style.

contents

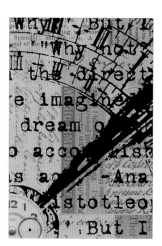

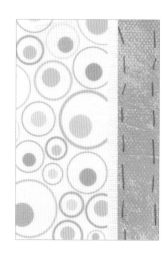

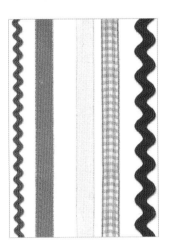

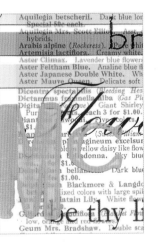

Please

AND THANK YOU

Every time I start a new scrapbook page, I ask myself the question, "what story do I want to share on this layout?" To me, one of the most exciting aspects of scrapbooking is combining my photographs, journaling and embellishments into a well-designed layout that tells a story.

As I wrote this book, I imagined myself sharing a story with you, a story about scrapbook page design. I found myself excited to write about design in a whole new way, taking traditional design principles and translating them into the language of scrapbooking. I want to help you understand how to decide what story you want to tell and then inspire you with powerful ways to creatively tell that story. And finally, I want you to feel comfortable and confident embracing your own personal style.

And so, my design story begins.

Edwards

A very special thank-you to *tina* Barriscale, *mellette* Berezoski, *joy* Bohon and *carrie* Colbert for their amazing talent, their dedication and most of all their friendship. To my *husband* and my *parents*, who never cease to supply me with amazing photos, hilarious stories, wonderful support and uninterrupted design time. And to my sweet *simon* boy, my everyday inspiration, for simply being himself.

tina Barriscale

mellette Berezoski

joy Bohon

carrie Colbert

THINK

before YOU
SPEAK

"Above all, stop and think what you are saying!"
— Emily Post

think
BEFORE YOU SPEAK

Think Before You Speak

How many of us grew up with our parents repeating that phrase? How many times have you stopped yourself before saying something you might have regretted, or given pause in order to collect your thoughts? In conversations and other methods of communication, thinking before you speak or write allows you to gather your *ideas* so you can convey them in the most *effective* way. It helps you to synthesize and get down to the core of what you really want to say, and allows you to say it in a way that's clear, respectful and to the point.

In designing scrapbook layouts, *stopping* and *thinking* before you begin gives you the opportunity to determine your overall vision for the page. It means slowing down and focusing on the message. What is it you want your layout to communicate years from now? What feelings do you want to evoke? Once you have a vision, you can begin constructing how you'll communicate (or design) that vision. That is what stopping and thinking is all about: *vision* and *communication*. These are two essential keys in the process of designing scrapbook pages.

SUPPLIES ON OPPOSITE PAGE *Page by Ali Edwards*
Patterned paper, transparencies, letter stickers and ruler sticker: K & Company; **Textured cardstock:** Bazzill Basics Paper; **Clock and "S" accent:** Li'l Davis Designs; **Acrylic paint and letter stamps:** Making Memories; **Rubber stamps:** Ma Vinci's Reliquary; **Stamping ink:** ColorBox Fluid Chalk, Clearsnap; **Pen:** American Crafts.

vision

Vision, also called *imagination*, is the beginning. It's the thinking before the speaking. It can be a single concept, such as the idea of "siblings," or it can be a completely designed layout you actually "see" in your mind. Vision is a mental image, a concept, an idea, a notion; vision is what motivates you to start working on a page.

My vision tends to begin with a story I want to tell. A pattern in my son's behavior I want to record. A memory my mom shared with me about my childhood. A thought about where I am in my life right now. At other times my vision begins when I open an envelope filled with new photographs. As I look through the images, certain ones stand out and speak to me in a special way. In an instant, visions begin to form in my mind. I'm motivated to tell a story through creative means, to share a memory with future generations.

Did you know that you are a visionary? You may be thinking, "Yeah, right." But it's true. You are a visionary—a person of great imagination simply because no one else sees the world the same way as you. Inside of you are stories waiting to be told. Your own visions. Your own points of view based on your unique life.

methods and manners

Writer and diarist Anaïs Nin said, "My ideas usually come not at my desk writing but in the midst of living." How true that is for me! Vision can strike at any time. Will you be ready? If you're like me, the only way to remember one of those sweet treats is to write it down immediately. Having paper and pen handy around the house, in the car and in my handbag has helped me remember so many ideas that I would have otherwise forgotten.

communication

Once you've established your vision, it's time to communicate (design) your message. Communication is how you choose to translate your vision into "real life." Sometimes a single word is the most powerful way to tell your story. In other cases, you may need to create a whole mini book in order to successfully communicate your vision. Through the use of words, photos, embellishments and design principles, you have the power to effectively tell your stories in so many creative ways.

Becoming a successful visual communicator is something you can learn. It can become a part of your personal process of recording your memories. Just as "please" and "thank you" come naturally, with a little time and effort, design principles can become so much a part of your creative process that you don't actively think of them as you're scrapbooking. This allows you to concentrate on communicating your story, on bringing your vision to life.

You can tell your story in endless ways. And there really is no right or wrong way to go about communicating that story.

In this chapter, I will teach you how to communicate your vision in three different ways: through design, words and photographs. As you read through this chapter, take a look at the vision (inspiration) of the page designers as well as the ways we've chosen to communicate that vision via our scrapbook layouts.

COMMUNICATING YOUR VISION THROUGH DESIGN

In this section, I teach you how to communicate your vision through design. Design can help you evoke a specific mood, can reinforce a theme, and can help you keep the focus on the most important parts of your layouts.

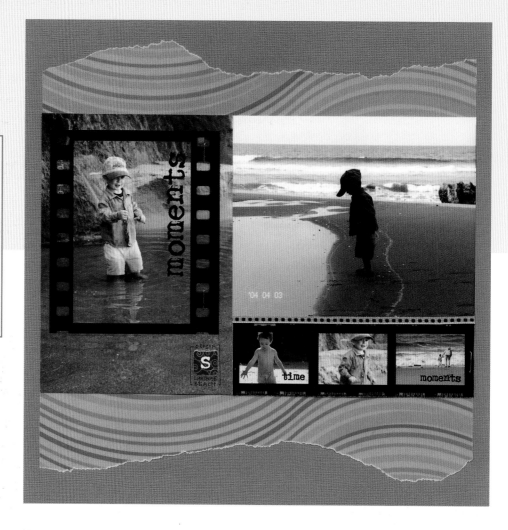

DESIGN TIP
Look to your photographs for elements of design you can repeat in your layouts. Lines and shapes are strong design elements that can be used to create repetition and movement on your pages.

Lighthouse Beach

vision | My original vision for this page began with the lines in the sand in the top-right photo. I love how Simon is standing between the line of the water and the former water line.

communication | The torn edges of the wavy-lined vellum was a natural choice for this layout, evoking the lines in the sand. My vision evolved to communicate the idea of moments—from the literal word "moments" written on the negative strip to each of the individual moments within the photos to the way the lines in the sand change in a matter of moments.

SUPPLIES *Page by Ali Edwards*
Patterned vellum: KI Memories; **Textured cardstock:** Bazzill Basics Paper; **Negative transparencies:** Narratives, Creative Imaginations; **Ribbon and rub-ons:** Making Memories; **Blue square sticker:** EK Success; **Pen:** Zig Millennium, EK Success; **Other:** Staples.

Roots

vision | This transparency inspired me to create a page based on the theme of "Roots."

communication | Working with a product that already communicates a message can inspire deeper journaling that relates to you.

additional ideas | Instead of creating a page with a full transparency, try cutting it up and using it across a two-page layout to tie the pages together. To create the word "Roots," I cut and layered individual letters on top of one another. I tucked hidden journaling and an additional photo under the long transparency piece on the second page.

SUPPLIES   *Pages by Ali Edwards*
Patterned paper and hinges: 7gypsies; **Textured cardstock:** Bazzill Basics Paper; **Handmade paper:** Artistic Scrapper; **Transparency:** Narratives, Creative Imaginations; **Vellum:** Autumn Leaves; **Slide holders:** Magic Scraps; **Ephemera:** me & my BIG ideas; **Letter charms and ribbon:** Making Memories; **Pen:** Zig Millennium, EK Success.

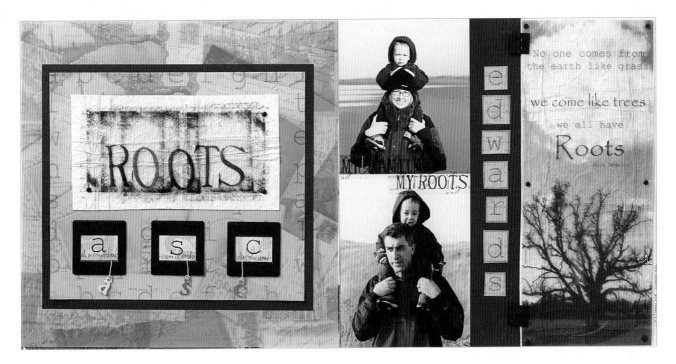

DESIGN TIP
Scrapbooking products (transparencies, printed paper, photo frames and so much more) are a great place to find inspiration for your pages. Choose a product that "speaks" to you and then translate it to your page.

How Much Do You Love Me ?

vision | Inspired by the 7gypsies patterned paper, Carrie wanted to capture the unconditional love she feels from Brad.

communication | To make the title words stand out on the patterned paper, Carrie carefully traced them with a gray pencil to create a shadow effect. To complement her paragraph-style journaling, she included word blocks around the photo, creating a unique photo mat that demonstrates Brad's various answers to her frequent question, "How much do you love me?"

SUPPLIES *Page by Carrie Colbert*
Patterned papers: Carolee's Creations and 7gypsies; **Heart embellishment:** Doodlebug Design; **Beaded embellishment:** EK Success; **Computer fonts:** Harting (journaling) and Dirty Ego (title), downloaded from the Internet.

Me and My Dad

vision | I wanted to create a page using my handwriting to create titles and accents.

communication | I scanned and printed my handwriting at different sizes to create the title and accents. The simple journaling communicates that in this case, the photos tell the story. This is particularly effective when you're working with photos from a time you don't remember.

additional idea | Don't be afraid of combining patterns. One of the simplest ways to combine patterns effectively is to choose patterns that are very close in color. The patterns on this page are busy but work well together because they're fairly neutral colors.

SUPPLIES   *Page by Ali Edwards*
Patterned papers: KI Memories and Anna Griffin; **Fabric paper:** me & my BIG ideas; **Metal flower accents:** Making Memories; **Computer font:** Adobe Garamond, downloaded from *www.adobe.com*.

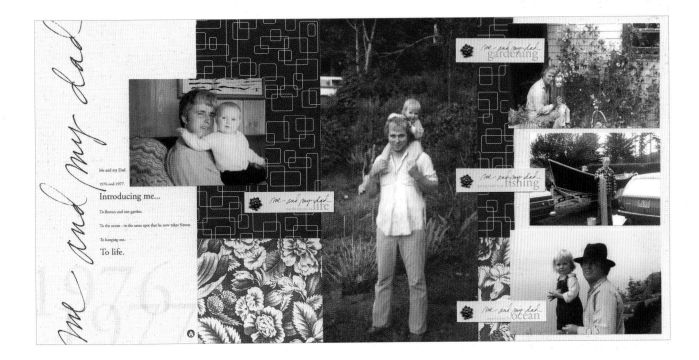

DESIGN TIP
Combine products, patterns, and styles on your page for a unique look.

"I am not a smart man, particularly, but one day, at long last, I stumbled from the dark woods of my own, and my family's, and my country's past, holding in my hands these truths: that love grows from the rich loam of forgiveness; that mongrels make good dogs; that the evidence of God exists in the roundness of things. I don't know much, but I know this much is true."
-Wally Lamb

Whole

vision | Tina's vision stemmed from a quilting technique—her layout uses graduated series of paper called *stratas*. The design is cut from these stratas and complemented by solid pieces of paper.

communication | Tina created her own design of interlocking small and large circles and semi-circles. The page flows whether the book is open, closed or if either of the flaps are open. She created four stratas of approximately 35 different patterned papers and graduated them from light to dark to light. Tina glued these strips to a long background and then divided the layout into twelve 6" blocks. Next she cut the shapes from the strata using a diagonal orientation, marked first with a compass. Using contrasting light and dark areas, Tina adhered the 6" blocks to the layout, adding the photos, embellishments and journaling printed on a transparency.

additional ideas | Tina used the circle pattern created by the design to illustrate the concept of "whole." Some of the circles are incomplete, yet they flow into other circles, illustrating the relationships described in the journaling.

SUPPLIES *Pages by Tina Barriscale*
Patterned papers: 7gypsies, Rusty Pickle, Karen Foster Design, K & Company, Sarah Lugg, Two Busy Moms, Creative Imaginations, Anna Griffin and Carolee's Creations; **Transparency:** Apollo; **Hinges and washer words:** Making Memories; **Round bookplate:** Li'l Davis Designs; **Number stamps:** A&P Numbers (small), Ma Vinci's Reliquary (large); **Stamping ink:** Memories, Stewart Superior Corporation; **Embossing powder:** Suze Weinberg; **Metallic rub-ons:** Craf-T Products; **Computer fonts:** LamboHmkBold (journaling) and Soli (title), downloaded from the Internet.

COMMUNICATING YOUR VISION THROUGH WORDS

In this section, I teach you how to communicate your vision through words. Finding your own voice as a storyteller is one of the best ways to communicate your vision. To find your voice, write like you talk or think. Communicate in a way that represents your true thoughts!

WHO? WHAT? WHERE? WHEN? WHY?

Just because. Because you are a KID. Because you are a BOY. Because you are TWO. Because this is what you are supposed to be doing. Because you enJOY climbing. Because you are an EXPLORER. Because it is sunny or rainy or hot or cold. Because it is fun. Because the grass was very green. BeCauSe there were rocks that were begging to be climbed. Because you are independent. Because your Dad loves to take photos just as much as your Mama Because you could. Because yOu Can

Why ?

vision | I wanted to create a page using a group of photographs that I took outside one afternoon.

communication | To communicate the feeling of these photos, I used a style of journaling that reflects how I felt watching Simon play on that particular day. To answer the question I posed with the title, I began my journaling with the word "Because." From there I let my thoughts (my distinct voice) continue the format of beginning each sentence with the same word to establish consistency and echo the pattern of the repetition of photos on the second page.

additional ideas | The small mini book on the second page includes more photos from this experience. Alternate computer journaling and letter stickers to add emphasis to particular words or phrases.

SUPPLIES *Pages by Ali Edwards*
Patterned paper: KI Memories; **Textured cardstock:** Bazzill Basics Paper; **Letter stamps:** Ma Vinci's Reliquary and PSX Design; **Letter stickers:** me & my BIG ideas; **Mini tags:** Making Memories; **Brads:** Two Peas in a Bucket; **Mini book:** Kolo; **Stickers:** Wordsworth; **Square punch:** Marvy Uchida; **"S" accent:** Li'l Davis Designs.

JOURNALING TIP
You don't always have to journal in full sentences (and your journaling doesn't need to be grammatically correct!). Try journaling with a few select words that express your feelings during a moment or event.

In 1985 my Mom penned a prayer to God asking for grace, patience and love in dealing with her children. Seeing her handwritten note, I think of how much God answered her prayer. She was and is the kindest, most loving and forgiving person I know. She helped us through our growing years – always available, always with a smile and a snack. Caring for us day and night. God certainly blessed her...and blessed us in the process.

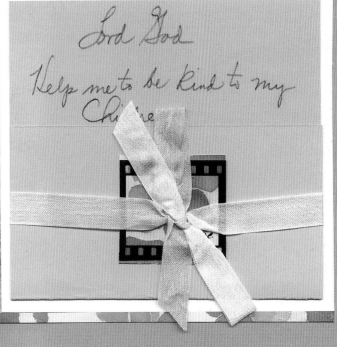

Pray

vision | I wanted to record a treasured prayer handwritten by my mom years ago.

communication | The best way to communicate my vision for this page was to scan my mother's prayer and print it out on colored cardstock. Seeing her handwriting communicates volumes to me and personalizes the memory.

SUPPLIES *Page by Ali Edwards*
Patterned paper: NRN Designs; **Textured cardstock:** Bazzill Basics Paper; **Brads:** Making Memories; **Negative strip:** Narratives, Creative Imaginations; **Ribbon:** 7gypsies; **Stamp copies:** Turtle Press.

Why?

vision | Mellette wanted to create a layout about the one word she's been hearing the most lately: "Why?"

communication | Because the "Why?" needed to be the most prominent part of the layout, Mellette created a frame around the large photo using the word "Why?" in different fonts.

SUPPLIES   *Page by Mellette Berezoski*
Patterned papers: Chatterbox and K & Company; **Molding strip, tag, letter stickers, rub-on, tacks and rivet:** Chatterbox; **Ephemera:** DMD, Inc.; **Wooden letters and ribbon:** Li'l Davis Designs; **Computer font:** CBX Trumpet, "Journaling Fonts" CD, Chatterbox.

How Do Lakes Become Ponds?

vision | Joy wanted to communicate a story about childhood memories and magic, and our changing perceptions as we age.

communication | Joy's words take you back in time. Her rich descriptions give a wonderful sense of place that are complemented by the photos. She weaves a tale with her words, taking you to the "lake" and then bringing you back to present day to visit the "ponds."

additional ideas | Joy made the first photo larger than the second to emphasize her view as a child. To add variety to the layout, Joy adhered part of the title to the second photo, which she positioned in the middle of her journaling. To create the frame, Joy applied embossing enamel to map paper for a watery look.

SUPPLIES *Pages by Joy Bohon*
Patterned paper: Rusty Pickle; **Transparency:** 3M; **Circle bookplate:** Li'l Davis Designs; **Metal rod:** K & Company; **Brads:** Lost Art Treasures; **Clips:** 7gypsies; **Stamping ink:** VersaMark, Tsukineko; **Embossing enamel:** Suze Weinberg; **Computer fonts:** Adler, Butterbrotpapier and Haettenschweiler, downloaded from the Internet.

Siblings

vision | My siblings and I have experienced so much together! When I found these pictures, I knew I wanted to create a mini book that would celebrate those relationships.

communication | Comparing photos from 20 years ago to 2002 allowed me to demonstrate the passage of time in our relationship. The combination of words, photos and cheerful patterned paper communicates a feeling of love, levity and celebration.

additional ideas | To create the foundation for this mini book, I glued two mini file folders together back to back. I covered the interior with patterned paper and vellum. Word stickers complement the color scheme.

SUPPLIES *Pages by Ali Edwards*
Patterned papers: K & Company; **Patterned vellum:** SEI; **File folders:** Rusty Pickle; **Fabric paper:** me & my BIG ideas; **Stickers:** Chatterbox; **String:** Making Memories; **Letter stamps:** PSX Design; **Number stamps:** Making Memories; **Stamping ink:** Ranger Industries and Hero Arts; **Bookplate:** Two Peas in a Bucket; **Pen:** Zig Millennium, EK Success; **Other:** Twill.

JOURNALING TIP
Struggling to create a vision based on words? Stop for a minute and let yourself feel the emotion behind your photographs. Let the emotion guide you as you begin to plan your scrapbook page.

pals

1982 Easter @
McDougall's

(M)

remembering

1980 north bend, oregon

unforgettable

Fast-forward 20 years. Twenty years of fun and tears, laughter and disagreements, swim-meets, golf tournaments, graduations, cars, weddings and births. So much experienced together... and apart. We sure do enjoy each-other these days. Always looking forward to the Next time together.

(s i B l i N g s)

special

1980 north bend, oregon

((fRi enDs))

2002 chip's wedding

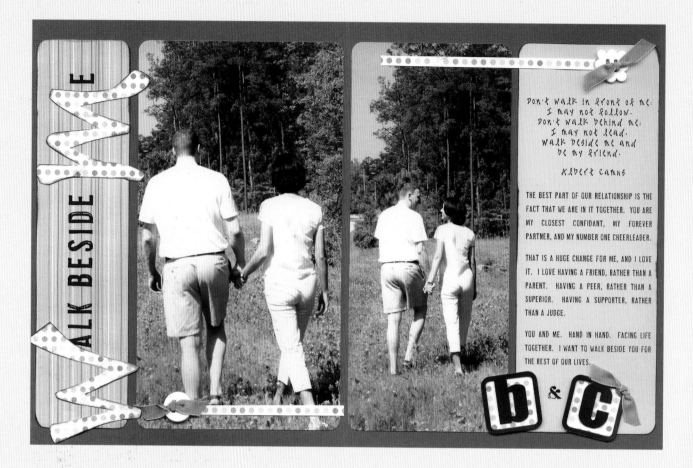

On the scrapbook layout:

WALK BESIDE ME

Don't walk in front of me:
I may not follow.
Don't walk behind me:
I may not lead.
Walk beside me and
be my friend.

Albert Camus

THE BEST PART OF OUR RELATIONSHIP IS THE FACT THAT WE ARE IN IT TOGETHER. YOU ARE MY CLOSEST CONFIDANT, MY FOREVER PARTNER, AND MY NUMBER ONE CHEERLEADER.

THAT IS A HUGE CHANGE FOR ME, AND I LOVE IT. I LOVE HAVING A FRIEND, RATHER THAN A PARENT. HAVING A PEER, RATHER THAN A SUPERIOR. HAVING A SUPPORTER, RATHER THAN A JUDGE.

YOU AND ME. HAND IN HAND. FACING LIFE TOGETHER. I WANT TO WALK BESIDE YOU FOR THE REST OF OUR LIVES.

b & c

Walk Beside Me

vision | Carrie wanted to capture how thankful she is to have found both a partner and a friend in Brad.

communication | To convey her vision for this layout Carrie paired a photo of Brad and herself walking hand in hand with a poem that speaks directly to this idea. To reinforce the idea of strength and stability, she incorporated strong vertical lines into the design, both through her use of patterned paper and the way in which she structured the vertical foundation (four vertical rectangles). The three matching ribbons form a nice visual triangle, keeping your eye focused within the page.

SUPPLIES *Pages by Carrie Colbert*
Patterned paper and acrylic accents: KI Memories; **Ribbon:** May Arts; **Metal letter clips:** Scrapworks; **Computer fonts:** AL Highlight and Messy G, downloaded from the Internet.

JOURNALING TIP
We most typically associate words with telling a story. Think about the stories you want to share with the people who will look at your scrapbook albums—and then communicate that story with words and design elements.

Doors

vision | I wanted to create a layout that highlights each of the places she's lived.

communication | Each of the tags on this page lifts to reveal a photo and a few comments about memories I have of that particular home. The phrase, the door patterned paper and the "opening" or lifting of each tag all communicate the idea of doors. I have always loved the phrase, "When one door closes, another opens," and it work well in this context where it's both literal and figurative.

additional ideas | By using a different color scheme for the words "door" and "opens," I draw attention to that phrase within the larger phrase.

SUPPLIES   *Page by Ali Edwards*
Patterned paper: Mustard Moon; **Patterned vellum:** Autumn Leaves; **Textured cardstock:** Bazzill Basics Paper; **Letters:** Mustard Moon; **Stamp stickers:** Scrappy Cat; **Rubber stamps:** PSX Design; **Stamping ink:** Clearsnap and Ranger Industries; **Pen:** American Crafts; **Snaps:** Making Memories; **Square tag:** Two Peas in a Bucket.

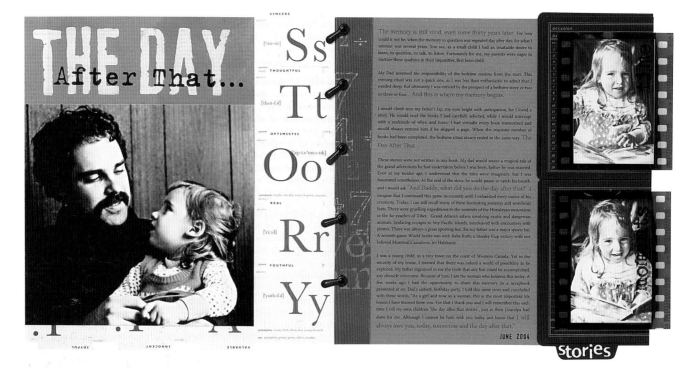

The Day After That Story

vision | Tina wanted to record memories, thoughts and feelings about a daily bedtime routine.

communication | This page powerfully communicates Tina's memories about the gift her father instilled in her. Her journaling brings us right into her room as a child and tells us exactly how important this ritual was in her life.

additional ideas | Tina placed the photos on the right-hand page on an Autumn Leaves folder, which she cut in half, placing one half on the top and one on the bottom vertically. Tina plans to have her dad write down some of the stories he told her as a child to insert in the folders.

SUPPLIES *Pages by Tina Barriscale*
Patterned paper: 7gypsies; **Transparency:** 3M; **Synonym tabs and file folders:** Autumn Leaves; **Rub-ons and negative holders:** Creative Imaginations; **Photo turns:** 7gypsies; **Tacks:** Chatterbox; **Foam stamps and acrylic paint:** Making Memories; **Computer font:** Warnock Pro Light, downloaded from the Internet.

COMMUNICATING YOUR VISION THROUGH PHOTOGRAPHS

As scrapbookers, our photographs are often the reason why we got started scrapbooking in the first place. My photographs are often my starting place for designing my vision. In this section of the chapter, I'll share ideas on how you can create and communicate a vision based on your photographs.

g o o f y

There are some photos that just make you laugh out loud. When I came across this one of Chris and Maria from 1979 I simply could not help myself. A priceless expression captured on film. A goofy moment between brother and sister. An oversized pair of red glasses. And me, twenty-some years later laughing. [journaled 5/18/04]

Goofy

PHOTOGRAPHY TIP
A "silly" photograph can often provide important insight into relationships, both past and current.

vision | I wanted to create a page that shares a silly photo of Chris and his sister.

communication | A one-word title set in proximity to the photo gets right to the point of the page. I could have easily chosen some wild patterned paper that reflects the silliness of the photo, but instead I went for stark white with their initials as accents.

SUPPLIES *Page by Ali Edwards*
Patterned Transparency: K & Company; **Accent letters:** Carolee's Creations; **Frames:** Design Originals; **Typewriter sticker:** Pixie Press; **Letter rub-ons:** Making Memories; **Computer font:** Myriad, downloaded from the Internet.

Collin

vision | I wanted to create a page focusing on photo memories of a high school boyfriend.

communication | On this layout, the photos take center stage in communicating my vision. I could write paragraph after paragraph about my relationship with Collin, but instead I briefly reflected back on our times together and let the photos do the rest of the talking.

additional ideas | Repeat the shapes of your photos to create an equal feeling between the two pages of a layout: here, the block of photos on the first page mimics the enlarged photo on the second page. Scrapbooking your own history is an important part of telling your story.

SUPPLIES   *Pages by Ali Edwards*
Patterned papers: Autumn Leaves and Making Memories; **Patterned vellum:** American Crafts; **Rub-ons:** Making Memories;
"C" sticker and square punch: Mrs. Grossman's; **Raised circle tag:** EK Success; **Pen:** Zig Millennium, EK Success.

Looking Back, Looking Forward

vision | As soon as Mellette saw the enlarged photo on this layout, she immediately thought of a paper her daughter had written for a creative writing class. Mellette wanted to capture the sentiments from that paper.

communication | Mellette enlarged her photo and printed it in color to emphasize her children's future together. To contrast the present and the past, she chose a few older photos of the two of them, which she printed at a reduced size in black and white. Mellette then added her daughter's creative writing paper.

additional ideas | Touches of green throughout the layout create balance and bring the eye back to the vision photograph.

SUPPLIES *Pages by Mellette Berezoski*
Patterned papers: Creative Imaginations, Chatterbox and 7gypsies; **Textured cardstock:** Bazzill Basics Paper; **Letter stickers:** SEI and Creative Imaginations; **Paper flowers, staples and ribbon:** Making Memories; **Number button:** EK Success; **Copper tag:** K & Company; **Rub-ons:** Creative Imaginations and Chatterbox; **Computer font:** Arial Narrow, Microsoft Word; **Other:** Charms.

You and Me

vision | I love these photographs that show how I interact with my son. I wanted to communicate the idea of "us," stemming from photos of Simon and me on a recent trip to the zoo.

communication | For this layout, I wanted to give equal weight to the words and the photos. One whole page is simply words, including a transparency that shows words I relate to my relationship with Simon. My journaling includes many of the things Simon and I enjoy doing together.

additional idea | Mat and frame a paint-stamped title to add emphasis. Add word stickers directly to photos to highlight emotions and feelings.

SUPPLIES *Page by Ali Edwards*
Patterned paper: Chatterbox; **Patterned vellum:** K & Company; **Textured cardstock:** Bazzill Basics Paper; **Word sticker:** Bo-Bunny Press; **Flower:** Carolee's Creations; **Acrylic paint and staples:** Making Memories; **Pen:** Staedtler.

> **PHOTOGRAPHY TIP**
> Look for photographs that show how you interact with loved ones on a daily basis.

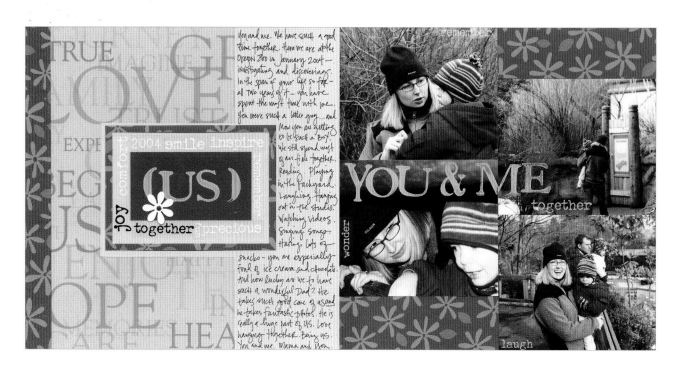

Perfect P

vision | Joy wanted to create a layout that describes Amelia's personality using several photos from the same event together with her daughter's initial.

communication | First Joy chose several photos that conveyed different personality traits of her daughter. She then created multiple text boxes and transparencies to showcase the variety of "P" words and letter forms.

PHOTOGRAPHY TIP
Look for a photographs that capture different aspects of your subjects' personalities and create pages that showcase their values, likes, dislikes, moods and emotions.

SUPPLIES   *Pages by Joy Bohon*
Patterned papers: Creative Imaginations and KI Memories; **Ribbon and photo turn:** 7gypsies; **Eyelet letter:** Making Memories; **Rub-on letters:** Li'l Davis Designs; **Letter tab:** Autumn Leaves; **Woven label:** me & my BIG ideas; **Transparencies:** 3M; **Computer fonts:** Dirty Ego, Casablanca Antique, Butterbrotpapier, Modern No. 20, Hattenschweiler, Adler, Trendy University, Blue Cake, Stamp Act, Ticket Capitals and Hootie, downloaded from the Internet; 2Peas Frazzled Stencil Negative, downloaded from *www.two-peasinabucket.com*.

Loving Life

vision | I wanted to create a page evoking Simon's constant movement and love for his boots.

communication | The horizontal orientation across the layout with the photos lined up side by side echoes the action and movement within the photos. The font also repeats the feeling of movement. The journaling, which speaks to Simon in the future, emphasizes his zest, sharing snippets of his childhood personality.

additional idea | I stamped the words "loving" and "entertain" in yellow first and then ran each section through my printer to add the words "always" and "life." You don't need a large-format printer to create this look—simply cut the cardstock to fit in your printer and then cover the seams with photos.

SUPPLIES   *Pages by Ali Edwards*
Patterned paper: Cross-My-Heart; **Textured cardstock:** Bazzill Basics Paper; **Stickers:** American Crafts; **Rubber stamps:** Making Memories; **"@" stamp:** Stampers Anonymous; **Stamping ink:** Clearsnap and Tsukineko; **Computer fonts:** P22 Cezanne, downloaded from *www.p22.com*; Orator, downloaded from the Internet.

#1 Son

vision | I wanted to create a layout based on Simon's "#1"-finger photo that communicates how he is our "#1."

communication | This page came together easily as I literally matched my journaling to my vision photo. To communicate my feelings that Simon is "#1," I thought about some of the things about his personality we love and used those ideas as my journaling.

additional idea | I created the journaling block for this layout using Macromedia Freehand. You can create the same look in Microsoft Word or Adobe Photoshop by using individual text boxes or layers.

SUPPLIES *Page by Ali Edwards*
Patterned papers: KI Memories and Scenic Route Paper Co.; **Metal circle:** K & Company; **Number stamp:** Ma Vinci's Reliquary; **Stamping ink:** ColorBox Fluid Chalk, Clearsnap; **Circle tag:** SEI.

PHOTOGRAPHY TIP
Look to your photographs for design ideas you can repeat on your page.

NUMBER

little dude
eater of plain brown bread
fan of the number 2
fan of his *B* (aka *bunny*)
organizer & sorter for age 2
Wiggles fan
shaka shaka dancer
rock collector
kitchen helper
SON

BUG

WONDERFUL

THOUGHTFUL

OPTIMISTIC

UNDERSTANDING

BUILDING A STRONG FOUNDATION. SOMETHING
FOR YOU TO BUILD UPON. IT IS ONE OF OUR
GOALS. TO GIVE YOU MORALS AND VALUES
AND MANNERS THAT YOU CAN BUILD UPON AS
YOU GROW AND DEVELOP INTO A MAN.
SOMEDAY YOU CAN TEACH THEM TO YOUR
OWN CHILDREN. THIS IS JUST THE BEGINNING.
YOU HAVE SO MANY CHOICES IN FRONT OF YOU
- SO MANY THINGS TO COME. BUT FOR NOW WE
BEGIN WITH THE BASICS:RESPECT, LOVE,
KINDNESS, AND A LITTLE BIT OF CHARM
THROWN IN FOR GOOD MEASURE.
IT BEGINS, SIMPLY, WITH A FOUNDATION.

LOVE

CHARMING

FOUNDATION

"Consideration for the rights and feelings of others is not merely a
rule for behavior in public but the very foundation upon
which social life is built."
— Emily Post

CHAPTER 2

BUILDING A STRONG

foundation

Defining Your Foundation

I'm one of those people who prefers everything to have a "home." My magazines have a *home* in a large wide basket with a tall handle. Our winter hats are kept in a long shallow basket that fits in the shelves of our mudroom. My rubber stamps safely reside (free from little fingers) within an old latch-top basket. *A place for everything and everything in its place* is definitely one of my personal mantras.

I look at my blank scrapbook pages in a similar manner. Once I formulate a vision in my mind, I assign each piece of my layout a "home" within a basic framework. This *framework* is my foundation. Your foundation serves as a placement guide for photos, journaling and embellishments. As you create a layout, you build upon this initial *foundation*, with the end goal of creating a page that communicates your story.

There are endless possibilities for building a solid foundation on a page. In this chapter, I share seven different ways to create a foundation on your page. I've included sketches and samples to illustrate each foundation so that you can learn how to build your own page.

SUPPLIES ON OPPOSITE PAGE   *Page by Ali Edwards*
Stitched paper and tags: Autumn Leaves; **Foam stamps and acrylic paint:** Making Memories; **"S" accent:** Li'l Davis Designs; **Computer fonts:** Bell Gothic (journaling), downloaded from the Internet; AL Patriot, package unknown, Autumn Leaves.

building your foundation

Building a foundation is as easy as deciding what you want the basic structure of your page to include. You can include as much or as little detail as you want. However, by deciding the foundation of your page before you start placing your page elements, you'll find designing a page easier and the end result will be more pleasing.

Joyful

vision | I wanted to create a layout that would celebrate the simple joys in my life.

communication | To communicate the concept of "simple joys," I used photographs, patterned paper and accents (the three circular elements include the initials of my immediate family members) to represent my favorite things. To balance out the straight lines on the second page, I used rub-on letters for my journaling.

SUPPLIES   *Page by Ali Edwards*
Patterned papers: Chatterbox, KI Memories, 7gypsies, The Paper Loft and K & Company; **Patterned vellum:** SEI; **Transparency:** Narratives, Creative Imaginations; **Typewriter accents:** Nostalgiques, EK Success; **Die-cut windows:** DieCuts with a View; **Word stickers:** Shotz, Creative Imaginations; **Rub-on letters:** Making Memories; **Letter stamps:** PSX Design; **Stamping ink:** Colorbox, Clearsnap; **Embossing powder:** Suze Weinberg; **Brads:** Two Peas in a Bucket; Stickers: Paperfever.

DESIGN IDEA
I based this layout on a template from *Die Cuts with a View*. Take a look at both sides of my sketch. Notice how the squares on both pages create "homes" for photographs and accents.

interpreting a basic foundation

Just as you can't know what a house will look like by simply looking at the foundation, you don't know what a scrapbook layout may look like from looking at a sketch. Color, texture, photo, and journaling choices all influence the look of a layout. On the following pages, I invited Tina, Mellette, Joy, and Carrie to use my sketch as the initial foundation for their pages. You'll find that their pages always look different from my pages, although we started with the same foundation.

tina | PAGE *47*   mellette | PAGE *39*   joy | PAGE *41*   carrie | PAGE *49*

methods and manners

I'm inclined to create foundations with straight lines. I'm a "line-it-up" type scrapper. I use a ruler, a craft knife and a lined self-healing mat to cut cardstock, crop photos and more. I measure distances on my page. This is all a part of my personal style.

But, some of my favorite scrapbookers create pages that appear to be less linear, with less of a visible, concrete structure. Even pages that appear to have very little in the way of a linear foundations are actually composed of a more complex underlying configuration. You can sometimes discover a hidden foundation by making a sketch of a page layout.

CREATE A FOUNDATION WITH PAGE TEMPLATES

Looking for a quick way to build a foundation on your page? I like using page templates and page die-cuts as a starting place. The die-cut pages provide me with a series of "homes," where I can place my photographs, accents and even my journaling.

Almost Two

vision | I wanted to showcase a variety of photographs of me from 1977.

communication | I layered two die-cut templates on top of each other to create a foundation similar to the sketch shown on the opposite page.

additional ideas | My mom always jotted down information on the back of my childhood photographs. When I was working on this page, I decided to scan an image of her handwriting to use as the page title.

SUPPLIES   *Page by Ali Edwards*
Patterned papers: KI Memories, Autumn Leaves and Anna Griffin; **Circle accents:** K & Company; **Ribbon:** Li'l Davis Designs;
Computer font: Goudy, downloaded from the Internet.

Flowers from Joe

mellette's interpretation | Notice how Mellette's photographs are cropped to the same size and shape as the photos on my layout. Also, notice how she gives the layout a different orientation by placing three horizontal tags across the left-hand side of the page.

SUPPLIES *Page by Mellette Berezoski*
Patterned papers: me & my BIG ideas, Chatterbox, Sweetwater, 7gypsies, KI Memories and K & Company; **Tag toppers:** KI Memories; **Decorative trim:** Nostalgiques, EK Success; **Ribbon, brads and photo anchors:** Making Memories; **Jump rings and button:** Junkitz; **Letter stickers:** K & Company; **Tags:** Stampin' Up! and DMD, Inc.; **Flower die cut:** Remember When; **Flower charms:** Two Peas in a Bucket; **Computer font:** AL Uncle Charles, package unknown, Autumn Leaves.

THE SKETCH
My sketch was inspired by a die-cut page template (*Perspectives by Making Memories*). Note the columns, the squares and the vertical placement of photographs in my sketch, as well as the placement of circular accents on the page.

CREATE A FOUNDATION THAT USES
THE ENTIRE SPACE ON YOUR LAYOUTS

As a designer, I often think of my cardstock as a blank foundation, divided up into quadrants of space.
I love the bold look of a layout that claims the entire space on a page, from edge to edge.

Boots

vision | Here's another pair of Simon's beloved boots! I love the story behind the pair of boots standing alone, in the mud!

communication | To create balance, I placed three photos in the bottom section of the second page, topped with three lines of journaling and two lines of ribbon. For the top section on the second page, I wanted to create a resting space so I simply added an embellishment with a close-up photo of the boots and the date. Did you notice this embellishment is lined up with the vertical line of the photo on the bottom? Alignment is an important consideration when placing elements within your foundation.

additional idea | Design inspiration is available everywhere! I drew inspiration from the lines in Simon's hat and repeated the look with ribbon and journaling.

SUPPLIES   *Pages by Ali Edwards*
Textured cardstock: Bazzill Basics Paper; **Magnetic letter stamps:** Making Memories; **Stamping ink:** Ranger Industries; **White rectangle:** KI Memories; **Ribbon:** May Arts; **Pen:** Zig Millennium, EK Success; **Computer fonts:** Myriad Bold and Myriad Condensed Bold, downloaded from the Internet.

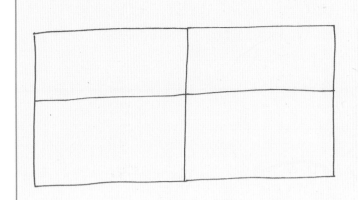

THE SKETCH

Notice how I placed the photographs and horizontal lines on this page. There is no space between the edge of the cardstock and the photographs, which joins them into a cohesive design unit. The foundation for this layout, which features elements stretching from one edge to the other, is essentially two 12" x 12" pages cut in half horizontally. Each of the four spaces holds an element.

Fear of the Tornado

joy's interpretation | Take a look at how Joy divided her cardstock into rectangular quadrants and how she filled each quadrant.

SUPPLIES *Page by Joy Bohon*
Patterned paper and clasp: 7gypsies; **Textured cardstock:** Bazzill Basics Paper; **Transparencies:** Creative Imaginations and 3M; **Puzzle piece:** Li'l Davis Designs; **Metal frame:** Scrapworks; **Epoxy number:** Creative Imaginations; **Rub-on letters:** Autumn Leaves; **Label maker:** Dymo; **Computer fonts:** Ticket Capitals and Casablanca, downloaded from the Internet; **Other:** Twill tape.

Coming Together

vision | I wanted to create a layout comparing and contrasting photographs of myself and my husband (as well as journal about the paths our lives have taken, as children and as adults, separately and together.)

communication | On this layout, the size and shape of the photos becomes a defining element of the foundation. Note that the title crosses over both pages, connecting the two sides together.

additional idea | I tucked my journaling underneath the scalloped edge along the bottom of the layout. To create the scallops, I punched randomly along the edge with a circle punch.

SUPPLIES   *Page by Ali Edwards*
Patterned papers: Anna Griffin and Laura Ashley; **Patterned vellum:** Nostalgiques, EK Success; **Handmade paper:** Artistic Scrapper; **Transparency, letter stickers and rub-ons:** Creative Imaginations; **Ribbon:** Making Memories; **Scrabble letters:** 7gypsies; **Brads:** Two Peas in a Bucket.

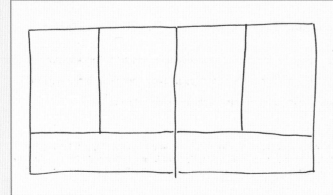

THE SKETCH
Here's another sketch that will teach you how to divide your page into rectangular quadrants. See how I've filled the page, edge to edge? Each page is made up of three basic areas: two rectangles on the top and one on the bottom.

my mini book interpretation | Are you starting to understand the concept of filling an entire page with photographs? You can use the same technique in a mini book. In this example, I've cropped and sized my photographs so that each photo fills an entire page of the book.

Jessica

vision | I used a mini book format to celebrate photos of my sister as an infant.

communication | Each page in this mini book becomes it's own foundation. Notice how I layered dates and text over each photograph (you can type information directly over your photographs using a program such as Adobe Photoshop).

SUPPLIES *Page by Ali Edwards*
Patterned papers: KI Memories and Making Memories; **Patterned vellum:** Autumn Leaves; **Mini book:** TidBits, Déjà Views, The C-Thru Ruler Co.; **Ribbon:** Making Memories and 7gypsies; **Frame charm:** Two Peas in a Bucket; **"J" letter tile:** DMD, Inc.; **Rub-on words:** Making Memories; **Word stickers:** Wordsworth; **4" circle sticker:** Li'l Davis Designs; **Pen:** Staedtler; **Computer font:** ITC Giovanni, downloaded from the Internet.

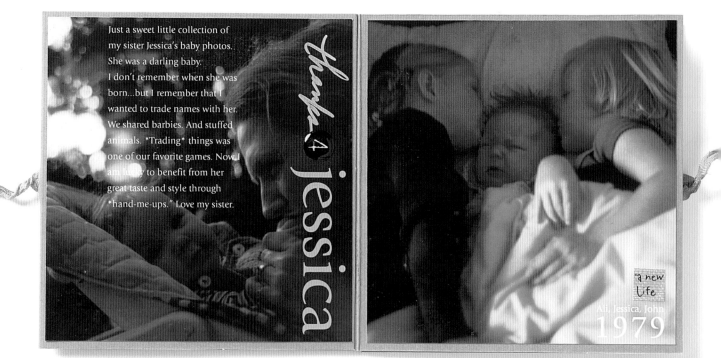

Just a sweet little collection of my sister Jessica's baby photos. She was a darling baby. I don't remember when she was born...but I remember that I wanted to trade names with her. We shared barbies. And stuffed animals. *Trading* things was one of our favorite games. Now I am lucky to benefit from her great taste and style through *hand-me-ups.* Love my sister.

thanks 4 jessica

a new life

Ali, Jessica, John

1979

love you

Grandma Cathy

1979

heaven's gift

coos bay, oregon

1980

step by step: "JESSICA"

This stylishly simple mini book can be used for any type of celebration or event—and, it makes a wonderful gift. Celebrate a friendship, a family member or a special weekend adventure ... the options are endless!

GATHER:

- A mini book
- Two patterned papers and one sheet of patterned vellum (*Note*: I chose to work with papers with a warm, orange tone and a contrasting brown paisley that ties in the blue of the mini book. I also chose these colors because the photos I'm working with are from the late 1970s/early 1980s—most of which have a warm hue.)
- One thin strip of ribbon for the cover and a thicker strip for the tie
- A letter tile for your subject's initial
- A frame that will fit the initial
- A number sticker
- Small rub-on words or stickers
- Four 5" x 5" photos (*Note*: I used Adobe Photoshop to scan, enlarge, crop and add text to my photos.)
- Large glue dots and other adhesives

CREATE:

COVER:

1. This mini book came with a sheet of white paper with a stock photo inside the window. Place the white sheet over your patterned paper and trim, using the square photo in the center as a template to cut the square from the middle. Do this for both the patterned paper and the vellum.

2. Adhere the patterned paper to the front of the book.

3. Add a rub-on word or sticker for your title.

4. Adhere the vellum over the top of the patterned paper.

INSIDE COVER:

1. Open up the mini book so the outside of the cover is lying flat on your work surface and the inside flap is open.

2. Using pliers, place and secure your letter tile inside the silver frame charm. (The charm I used has four prongs on the back that hold the tile in place.)

3. String the frame charm onto the thin strip of ribbon.

4. Lay the ribbon and charm face down in the center of the square. Adhere the two ends of the ribbon to the inside of the cover with tape or another adhesive. Lift up your book to make sure the ribbon charm is centered and place back down again.

5. Adhere a large glue dot to the back of the charm and tile.

6. Cut a square of the brown paisley paper that's large enough to cover the window and adhere to the inside of the flap.

7. Using a craft knife, make a slit in the crease between the cover and the flap that's large enough for your ribbon to fit through.

8. Slide the ribbon through and adhere the end of the ribbon to the inside of the cover.

9. Adhere the inside of the flap to the back of the cover. This will hide all the interior gluing you did in the previous steps.

PAGES:

1. Adhere your photos to the four inside pages.

2. Adhere word stickers to some of the remaining patterned paper and place above the date/text information on your photos.

3. Using a craft knife, make a slit in the crease between the second to the last and the last page that's large enough for your ribbon to fit through.

4. Slide the ribbon through and adhere (the spot you adhere the ribbon to will be hidden once the page is glued).

5. Glue the backs of the pages together so that when you're finished you have four pages of photos.

CREATE A FOUNDATION BASED ON THREE ELEMENTS

In the previous section, I taught you how to create foundations based on elements that go edge to edge on a page. Here I'll teach you how to create a foundation within your page using three elements.

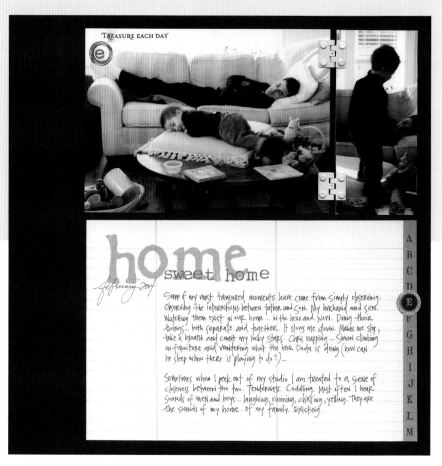

Home Sweet Home

vision | I loved how these less than perfect, yet still precious, photographs captured an "everyday" moment in the life of my family.

communication | Notice how I placed my photographs inside of the structure of my foundation. One of the photos shows more of the situation—the room, Chris's and Simon's full bodies, etc. The second photo is cropped and focuses on Simon looking at Chris. To visually connect the foundation photos, I attached hinges to them.

additional ideas | If you want to hand-journal but are concerned about writing in straight lines, try some of the cool lined papers available. Remember to journal about your role as an observer in your life. What do you see daily in your home? What is real life like for you? For your loved ones?

SUPPLIES *Page by Ali Edwards*
Patterned papers: KI Memories and Making Memories; **Rubber stamps:** Ma Vinci's Reliquary and PSX Design; **Stamping ink:** Memories, Steart Superior Corporation; **Rub-ons and hinges:** Making Memories; **Circle stickers:** EK Success (under "e"), Creative Imaginations ("e"); **Pen:** Zig Millennium, EK Success.

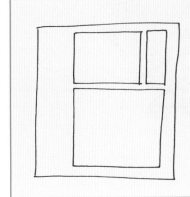

THE SKETCH
The foundation of this sketch consists of three elements: two horizontal shapes and one vertical shape. Notice how the space between the three shapes is even. Also, notice that the foundation for this layout is not placed squarely in the middle of the page.

2 in Review

tina's interpretation | Notice how Tina increased the size of the bottom block so that she could add more photographs to her page. When you look at Tina's page, you see eight photographs and several accents—yet, notice how the main section of her layout is composed of three elements.

SUPPLIES *Page by Tina Barriscale*
Patterned papers: KI Memories (blue), Chatterbox (white floral); **Foam stamps and acrylic paint:** Making Memories; **2" typewriter-key number:** Nostalgiques, EK Success; **Wooden letters and numbers:** Li'l Davis Designs; **Tinker pins:** 7gypsies; **Index tabs:** KI Memories; **Staples:** Office Depot; **Computer font:** Scala Sans, downloaded from the Internet.

CREATE A FOUNDATION BY PAINTING OR DRAWING YOUR OWN OUTLINE GRID

I love being able to "build" a foundation on my page by simply painting or drawing lines onto cardstock. Can't draw a straight line? No worries! You can create an outline grid that's deliberately non-linear (or consider using products such as page templates to create a perfectly linear look.)

Today You

vision | Simon's mornings are always full! I wanted to create a layout that shared a glimpse into a day in his life.

communication | For this layout, I created my own foundation by painting lines on cardstock. The resulting rectangles hold journaling and photographs. Notice how some of the photos break out of their "homes"—just because you create a visible foundation doesn't mean your information has to stay within the lines. Notice how all of the white words are lined up horizontally across both pages. This is another way to add structure and seems to work particularly well on this layout as a contrast to the hand-painted lines.

SUPPLIES *Page by Ali Edwards*
Patterned paper: Scenic Route Paper Co.; **Textured cardstock:** Bazzill Basics Paper; **Letter stamps and acrylic paint:** Making Memories; **Tabs:** Autumn Leaves; **Pen:** American Crafts.

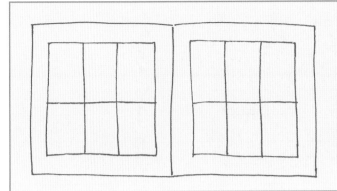

THE SKETCH
I drew a series of rectangles in different sizes and shapes, with the intention that each rectangle would hold a photograph, journaling, and/or an accent.

European Memories

carrie's interpretation | Notice how Carrie used word stickers to create the outline of her page foundation.

SUPPLIES *Page by Carrie Colbert*
Letter stickers: The Paper Loft; **Clay accents:** Li'l Davis Designs; **Leather lines and word stickers:** Making Memories; **Computer font:** AL Uncle Charles, package uknown, Autumn Leaves.

CREATE A FOUNDATION BASED ON A VERTICAL COLUMN

When I'm creating a simple page, I often like to create a page foundation based on a vertical column. It's easy to align a combination of elements with one column.

Aidan

vision | My vision for this page began with the photos and my feelings about first-time motherhood.

communication | The position of the photos in a vertical orientation creates a home for the stamped phrases and the square embellishment in the center. In addition, the large stamps serve to hold that important information in place, giving even more structure to the overall page.

additional ideas | When I'm creating a relatively simple page like this, I like to choose photos and embellishments that make a big impact. Tightly cropped photos, a strong contrast in color and layered embellishments are great ways to draw attention.

SUPPLIES   *Page by Ali Edwards*
Textured cardstock: Bazzill Basics Paper; **Foam stamps and acrylic paint:** Making Memories; **Letter stamps:** PSX Design; **Woven label:** me & my BIG ideas; **Wire connector:** 7gypsies; **Die-cut square:** Carolee's Creations.

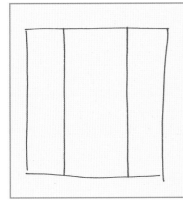

THE SKETCH
Notice how I sketched various page elements within a vertical column. This sketch is so easy to adapt to your own embellishments!

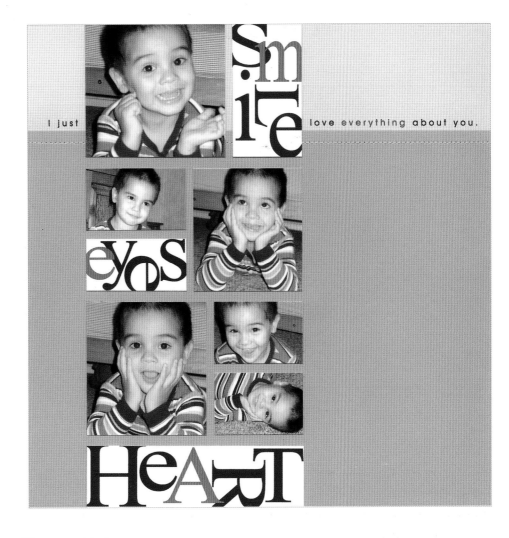

I just **SmiLe** love everything about you.

eyes

HeART

Everything

mellette's interpretation | Notice how she used text to fill the spaces that don't have photographs. She also moved her column towards the left-hand side of her cardstock.

SUPPLIES *Page by Mellette Berezoski*
Textured cardstock: Bazzill Basics Paper; **Computer fonts:** Times New Roman and Avant Garde, Microsoft Word.

a two page interpretation | Now that you've mastered a vertical foundation on one page, here's how to apply the same principle to a two-page spread.

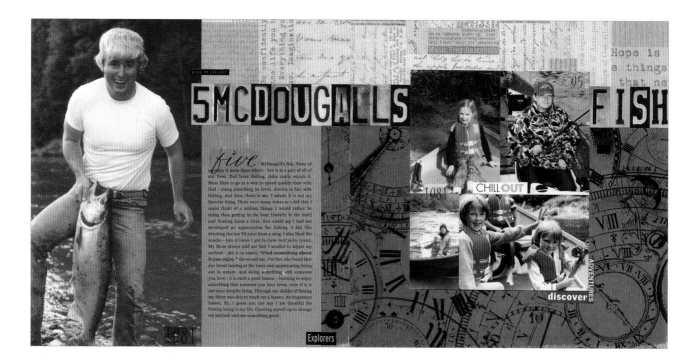

Fish

vision | My mom taught me so many important lessons. On this layout, I wanted to share a valuable lesson that I learned about fishing.

communication | When creating a foundation for a two-page layout, it's important to look at both pages as a single layout. A foundation with shapes that cross over from one page to the other makes a very stable layout. Part of the fun of creating a foundation is finding ways to break out of the structure. Notice how the first letter of the title crosses over the line created by the main photo—this helps connect the first photo with the photo block on the second page. This idea of breaking across a hard line is repeated by two smaller word stickers on the first page.

SUPPLIES   *Page by Ali Edwards*
Patterned paper and transparency: K & Company; **Letter stickers:** The Paper Loft; **Word stickers:** Making Memories; **Number sticker:** Bo-Bunny Press; **Computer font:** Georgia, Microsoft Word.

CREATE A FOUNDATION BASED ON PAGE COMPARTMENTS

When building a foundation for your page, you can think in terms of one big page foundation—or you can also separate your page into compartments. Compartments can add organizational structure to your page by grouping related bits of information (photographs, journaling and embellishments can all fit neatly into compartments) into a cohesive structure.

My Quirks

vision | I wanted to highlight a funny photo of me taken by a friend.

communication | On this page, I stamped small blocks and filled them with small bits of journaling. I used a paisley print piece of fabric behind the photo and title block.

additional ideas | Who are you? What's funny about you? Record some of your quirks.

SUPPLIES *Page by Ali Edwards, Photo by Tara Whitney*
Patterned paper: me & my BIG ideas; **Textured cardstock:** Bazzill Basics Paper; **Ribbon:** Li'l Davis Designs; **Rubber stamps:** Stamp It (large square), PSX Design ("First Class"), EK Success ("A"); **Stamping ink:** Ranger Industries; **Corner punch:** Marvy Uchida; **Vellum quote:** Déjà Views, The C-Thru Ruler Co.; **Square clip:** Nostalgiques, EK Success; **Fabric:** 3 Sisters.

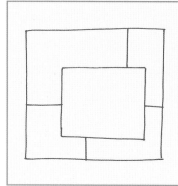

THE SKETCH
Notice how I created the compartments on this page. I used a series of seven squares on the left hand side of my layout to create individual "homes" for page elements. I added a second compartment by sketching in a large rectangular block for a photograph/title element.

Brad the Photographer

carrie's interpretation | Notice how Carrie expanded the basic idea to a two-page spread.

SUPPLIES *Pages by Carrie Colbert*
Patterned paper: Anna Griffin; **Canvas embellishment and epoxy letters:** Li'l Davis Designs; **Letter rub-ons:** Creative Imaginations; **Computer font:** Twentieth Century Condensed, downloaded from the Internet.

Brad the photographer

sMiLe

I love scrapbooking! That is no secret. What may be a secret though is that I am not a very good photographer! There, I admitted it. Now that could potentially pose a problem since photos are essential to my hobby. But it doesn't for me because I have Brad! His knowledge and love for photography fits perfectly with my passion for preserving memories. He is my personal photographer. For instance, when we are on vacation and an important photo opportunity presents itself, he is my go-to man. While I may take a stab at capturing the memories, he is my sure bet for a good photo. Yet another way in which we are a perfect match, and yet another reason I am thankful for him. ☺ {2004}

CREATE A FOUNDATION WITH CARDSTOCK AND/OR PATTERNED PAPER

One of my favorite ways to build a foundation for a two-page layout is to simply cut a sheet of cardstock in half and place one half on one page and the other half on the second page. From that basic starting point, you can build more complicated structures (add compartments, use page templates, add a vertical column).

Give Thanks

vision | I wanted to create a layout to celebrate my memories of Halloween in 1982.

communication | Notice how I placed my photographs in a quadrant on the left-hand side of my layout. The arrow in the middle of the first page literally directs your eye to page two.

SUPPLIES *Pages by Ali Edwards*
Patterned papers: Chatterbox, The Paper Loft and Autumn Leaves; **Woven label:** me & my BIG ideas; **Foam stamps, fabric photo corner and rub-ons:** Making Memories; **Domed letters:** Rusty Pickle; **Stamping ink:** StazOn, Tsukineko; **Pen:** Zig Millennium, EK Success.

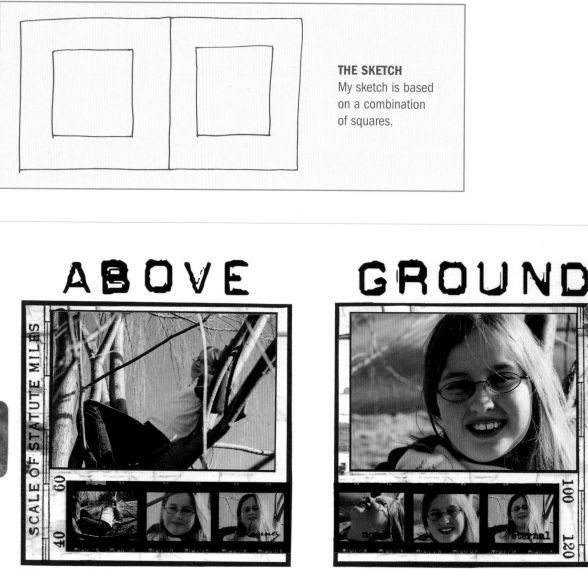

Above Ground

joy's interpretation | I asked Joy to create a layout based on my sketch. Notice
how she modified the sketch, adding a large photograph to each half of her layout and
using small square photographs as a border on each page.

SUPPLIES   *Pages by Joy Bohon*
Patterned paper: Mustard Moon; **Textured cardstock:** Chatterbox and Bazzill Basics Paper; **Transparencies:** Creative
Imaginations and 3M; **Filmstrips:** Creative Imaginations; **Wooden number:** Li'l Davis Designs; **Metal bars:** 7gypsies;
Computer fonts: Adler and GF Ordner Inverted, downloaded from the Internet.

a patterned paper interpretation | *Now that you've learned how to create a foundation with cardstock, here's an example of how you can create a foundation with patterned paper.*

A&P

vision | I wanted to create a page highlighting my parents in the early part of their relationship.

communication | The foundation for this layout is made up of three sections of patterned paper, which creates a background for the essential information on top. The white borders around the photos act as highlighters, with the word stickers acting as titles for each individual photo.

additional ideas | Who are, or were, your parents? What were they like in the beginning of their relationship? Take some time to record their stories.

SUPPLIES   *Pages by Ali Edwards*
Patterned papers: Anna Griffin (stripes), Mustard Moon (text); **Textured cardstock:** Bazzill Basics Paper; **Patterned vellum:** Autumn Leaves; **Circle accents:** KI Memories; **Brads, letter stamps, acrylic paint and letter charms:** Making Memories; **Twill words:** All My Memories; **Pen:** Zig Millennium, EK Success; **Photo paper:** Epson; **Circle punch:** Punch Bunch.

BEYOND THIS PAGE: *using foundations on greeting cards*

As I've shared in this chapter, I love using foundations to create "homes" for elements on my scrapbook pages. I also like to use this technique when I make cards to share with my friends and family members. Here's an example.

Live

vision | I wanted to create a card that shares thoughts about my married life.

communication | Notice the two vertical columns on the inside of the card. I filled the first column by placing five punched rectangles in the left-hand column. I created a home for my title by placing the word "live" inside a metal bookplate.

additional ideas | To convey the passage of time, I layered a clock transparency over the front of the card and repeated a piece of the same transparency inside my card. Also, I punched the rectangular embellishments from monochromatic patterned paper. There are so many amazing patterned papers available, and it's easy to mix and match when you choose different patterns from the same color family.

SUPPLIES *Pages by Ali Edwards*
Patterned papers: Anna Griffin (stripes), Mustard Moon (text); **Textured cardstock:** Bazzill Basics Paper; **Patterned vellum:** Autumn Leaves; **Circle accents:** KI Memories; **Brads, letter stamps, acrylic paint and letter charms:** Making Memories; **Twill words:** All My Memories; **Pen:** Zig Millennium, EK Success; **Photo paper:** Epson; **Circle punch:** Punch Bunch.

chapter Checklist

7 WAYS TO CREATE A FOUNDATION ON YOUR LAYOUTS

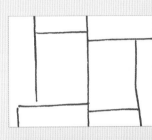
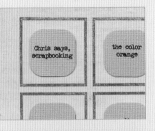

1. *Use a page template.*

2. *Fill all of the space on your page*

3. *Create a foundation based on three elements.*

4. *Start with a vertical column.*

5. *Draw or paint an outline grid.*

6. *Create page compartments.*

7. *Use cardstock/patterned paper.*

getting together. sharing time
and moments and laughter.
How lucky am I to have Jim
and Kathy in my life—thank you
John for finding such a wonderful
spouse...with such a special, fun
loving family.
Good people
who are open
to sharing
their lives.
Gatherings.
Friends. Family.
Connections.

GATHERING
together

"Above all, at any gathering 'hospitality makes for infectious fun.'"
— Kate Spade

gathering TOGETHER

Coming Together

Ah, gatherings. A coming together of friends and family. I love the laughter, the reminiscing, the *togetherness*. Gathering with my friends and family is one of my favorite things to do!

Just as I love gathering my friends and family together, I also enjoy gathering objects together to create a certain look and feel on my scrapbook pages. When I design a page, I like to *repeat* similar elements to create visual impact. In design, a gathering is how you *combine* different elements on a page to create a look that communicates the story you want to share on your scrapbook page.

Creating *gatherings* on my layouts is one of my favorite design techniques. It must be the organizer in me that likes to see the structure inherent in the repetition of objects!

In this chapter, I'll teach you my favorite strategies for creating gatherings based on embellishments, patterned paper, photographs and words.

}

SUPPLIES ON OPPOSITE PAGE *Page by Ali Edwards*
Patterned paper: Creative Imaginations; **Fabric paper:** me & my BIG ideas; **Textured cardstock:** Bazzill Basics Paper; **Rubber stamps:** Just for Fun (square), Making Memories (foam letters and flower), EK Success (circle letters); **Acrylic paint and brad:** Making Memories; **Pen:** American Crafts.

THREE WAYS TO GATHER
EMBELLISHMENTS ON YOUR LAYOUTS

In this section, I will show you several ways to group embellishments—stamped images, punched shapes and metal embellishments—on your layouts.

stamped images

I love the look of stamped images on a layout. It's so easy to combine alphabet stamps and other images.

Life Moments

vision | The photo on the first page spoke to me as such a perfect glimpse of a quiet moment in Simon's life.

communication | For my gathering, I stamped the rectangle boxes and the letters of Simon's name, and then added the woven labels vertically within the boxes. The orange color of the middle label is repeated in the door of our home (first photo) and also in the color of cardstock I chose for the journaling.

additional idea | Rub-on letters stick to anything and everything! Here I attached a white "S" to the top of a KI Memories Icicle accent to create an initial embellishment.

SUPPLIES *Page by Ali Edwards*
Patterned papers: 7gypsies (words), Rusty Pickle (letters); **Transparency:** Creative Imaginations; **Patterned vellum:** Heidi Grace Designs; **Textured cardstock:** Bazzill Basics Paper; **Square accents:** KI Memories; **Rub-ons:** Autumn Leaves; **Pins:** Making Memories; **Woven labels:** me & my BIG ideas; **Rectangle stamp:** Stamp It; **Letter stamps:** Making Memories; **Stamping ink:** ColorBox, Clearsnap; **Computer font:** AL Post, package unknown, Autumn Leaves.

Swim, Swim

vision | I wanted to create a page using photos from a variety of swimming events and activities.

communication | Notice how I paired a gathering of stamped images with a gathering of photographs on this page. Don't be afraid to interchange ink and paint. For the stamped "swim" section, I combined inks and paints based on the colors I had available.

SUPPLIES   *Page by Ali Edwards*
Textured cardstock: Bazzill Basics Paper; **Rubber stamps:** Ma Vinci's Reliquary; **Stamping ink:** ColorBox, Clearsnap; **Acrylic paint:** Making Memories; **Rub-ons:** Autumn Leaves and Making Memories; **Letter stickers:** K & Company; **Pen:** American Crafts.

Party of 4

vision | Mellette wanted to create a page that shows the different personalities of her children and their cousins.

communication | Mellette divided the layout so that a different patterned paper, embellishment and fonts represent each child. She repeatedly stamped the number "4" with four different stamps and ink/paint colors, creating her own patterned paper to help emphasize the theme and title. She placed the individual photos and journaling randomly throughout each child's "section" to help create a fun, whimsical feel. Notice that even the random stitching helps create a playful mood.

SUPPLIES   *Page by Mellette Berezoski*

Patterned papers: Making Memories, Chatterbox and Rusty Pickle; **Number stamps:** Making Memories and Ma Vinci's Reliquary; **Acrylic paint, metal letters and bookplate:** Making Memories; **Rub-on letters:** Making Memories and Chatterbox; **Letter tiles:** Junkitz; **Index tab:** Sweetwater; **Button:** Karen Foster Design; **Ribbon:** K & Company and C.M. Offray & Son; **Labels:** Dymo; **Computer fonts:** 2Peas Air Plane, 2Peas Miss Happy, 2Peas Shake and 2Peas Stop Sign, downloaded from twopeasinabucket.com.

punched shapes

My square, rectangle and circle punches are some of my favorite tools. The small shapes are perfect for creating design elements, such as borders, on my scrapbook pages.

1980 Christmas

vision | I wanted to celebrate Christmas memories from 1980.

communication | The gatherings of punches on this layout are placed vertically, acting as borders for the spread. The journaling is focused on a specific memory (the bikes), while the other photos assist in creating a larger "picture" of the holiday.

additional idea | I created the "1980" on the main photo by placing number stickers on top of the photo that I printed and then peeling them off.

SUPPLIES *Pages by Ali Edwards*
Patterned papers: Anna Griffin, 7gypsies and Autumn Leaves; **Rub-on:** Making Memories; **Transparencies:** Narratives, Creative Imaginations; **Photo turns:** 7gypsies; **"M" charm:** DieCuts with a View; **Brads:** Two Peas in a Bucket; **Woven label:** me & my BIG ideas; **Letter stickers:** SEI; **Stamp punch:** McGill; **Computer font:** Avant Garde, downloaded from the Internet.

Celebration

vision | The "Celebration" transparency was my original inspiration for this page. While playing around on my scrap table, I had a "happy accident," where some punched circles landed under the transparency creating a look similar to confetti.

communication | I punched several circles of the same size from two sheets of patterned paper and placed them underneath the transparency in clusters. I adhered each punched circle to the foundation and covered it with the transparency. On the first page, I placed one of the photos under the transparency, and placed the other two where the transparency was cut.

additional ideas | When scrapbooking past events, sometimes all you have to work with is blurry photos. Select the best photo to emphasize and use the rest to communicate a general feeling about the event.

SUPPLIES   *Pages by Ali Edwards*
Patterned paper: Chatterbox; **Transparency:** Daisy D's Paper Co.; **Foam stamps, snaps and acrylic paint:** Making Memories;
"Memories" sticker: Bo-Bunny Press; **Computer font:** Ghostwriter, downloaded from the Internet.

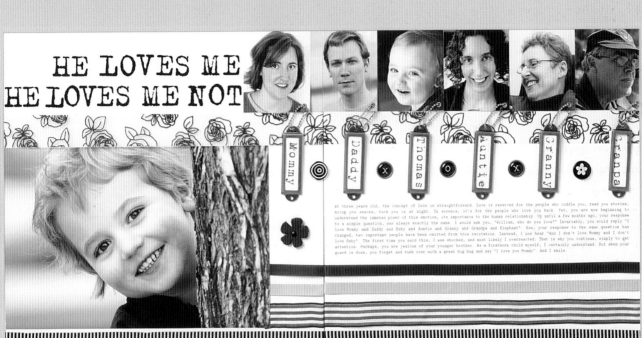

He Loves Me, He Loves Me Not

vision | Tina wanted to record the growth of her son's understanding of love.

communication | Notice how Tina created a border with the metal bookplates on her layout. Tina used the floral ribbon to continue the "loves me, loves me not" theme of the page and incorporated two additional flower embellishments, repeating the red and black accent theme.

additional ideas | One of my favorite aspects of this page is the journaling. Not only does it look at William's changing perceptions of his own life, but it shares Tina's reactions and feelings as well. Such a great example of real life journaling!

DESIGN IDEA
I love filling metal frames and book-plates with text (and/or photographs!) to create embellishments that are unique to my page.

SUPPLIES *Pages by Tina Barriscale*
Rub-ons, bookplates, leather flower, eyelets and beaded chain: Making Memories; **Black tack:** Chatterbox; **Acrylic accents:** KI Memories; **Bubble letters and frames:** Li'l Davis Designs; **Computer font:** Isotype, downloaded from the Internet; **Other:** Ribbon.

THREE STRATEGIES FOR COMBINING PATTERNED PAPERS ON YOUR LAYOUTS

As a scrapbooker designer, I enjoy the challenge of combining two or more different patterned papers on my layouts. In this section, I'll teach you my strategies for combining patterned papers together in an eye-appealing way.

color blocks

Color blocking is an easy way to incorporate different types of patterned papers on your layouts. Look to your photographs for colors to feature on your layout. Another tip? For easy color-matching, look for coordinated prints from the same company.

Simple Pink Delight

vision | As a child, my favorite color was pink! As an adult, I'm now happily wearing pink again. I wanted to highlight photos of me as a child in pink clothing while reflecting on the fact that it's still a favorite color for me today.

communication | Gatherings can consist of large blocks of color to set a tone or mood for your layout. In this case, the pink blocks repeat the pink colors found on my clothes in the photos. I chose to place a title on one block, some journaling and a photo on another, and photos on the other two.

SUPPLIES   *Pages by Ali Edwards*
Patterned papers: Chatterbox and Autumn Leaves; **Patterned vellum:** SEI; **Rub-ons and brad:** Making Memories; **Canvas frame:** Li'l Davis Designs; **"A" card:** Autumn Leaves; **Other:** Ribbon.

color repetition

Another strategy for combining color and patterned paper? Choose patterned papers (a striped print, a paisley print, a text-inspired print) that have the same background color and then look for opportunities to repeat that color in other elements of your page.

Celebrating Freedom

vision | Mellette wanted to celebrate the feelings of freedom and love of family on the Fourth of July.

communication | Focusing on the color red (which lends a patriotic feel to the layout), Mellette stitched together four different red patterned papers along the right side to help ground the small photos and journaling block. She changed the small photos to black and white so the distracting background and assorted colors didn't compete with the busy patterned papers. Notice that the other red elements on the page form a visual triangle to help balance out the large red strip.

SUPPLIES   *Page by Mellette Berezoski*
Patterned papers: Chatterbox, 7gypsies, Anna Griffin and Daisy D's Paper Co.; **Stitched tag, round clear tag, rub-on letters, letter stickers, word sticker, molding, eyelets and tacks:** Chatterbox; **Acrylic tile:** Junkitz; **Pens:** American Crafts; **Photo corners:** Kolo; **Letter stamps:** Making Memories; **Acrylic paint:** Plaid Enterprises; **Computer font:** CBX Watson, "Journaling Fonts" CD, Chatterbox; **Other:** Ribbon and string.

quadrant placement

In a previous chapter, I encouraged you to think of your page foundation in terms of quadrants. This technique is also a good way to combine patterned paper on your layouts. Think about dividing your cardstock into four equal quadrants, and fill two or three of the quadrants with patterned paper.

The Francis Wedding

vision | Carrie wanted to create a layout that showcased the beautiful professional pictures she ordered from her friend's wedding.

communication | Notice how Carrie divided her layout into four quadrants. She placed patterned paper on the upper right and lower left-hand corners of the layout.

additional ideas | In addition to combining different patterned papers on her layout, Carrie also created a grouping by using three 4"x 6" black and white photographs. Look at her photo placement and how the three black and white photographs seem to create a unified group.

SUPPLIES   *Pages by Carrie Colbert*
Patterned papers: Anna Griffin and K & Company; **Title rub-ons and leather frames:** Making Memories; **Title epoxy stickers, wooden flowers and date ticket:** Li'l Davis Designs; **Transparencies:** Narratives, Creative Imaginations.

THREE WAYS TO GATHER WORDS ON YOUR LAYOUTS

I love words—not just for journaling, but also as an important design element on my page. When you think about words as a design element, think about rub-on letters, stickers, computer fonts, and yes, even your own handwriting. Here are three ways to effectively use words as a design element on your pages.

word stickers

It's easy to group small word stickers together to create a title and/or a design element for your page.

Little Things

vision | Guided by the enlarged photo, my goal was to highlight a few of the little things we love about Simon.

communication | To create the accent on my page, I started with a negative frame. I then cut and layered word stickers inside the frame to create an accent that reveals why Simon is "my boy."

SUPPLIES   *Page by Ali Edwards*
Patterned paper: David Walker, Creative Imaginations; **Textured cardstock:** Bazzill Basics Paper; **Rub-on letters:** Li'l Davis Designs; **Transparency:** Creative Imaginations; **"S" clip:** Nostalgiques, EK Success; **Word stickers and acrylic paint:** Making Memories; **Pen:** American Crafts; **Other:** Staples.

font combinations

I enjoy mixing fonts and rubber stamps to create a custom look for my pages. Don't be afraid to experiment with different combinations of letters to create unique looks for your own layouts.

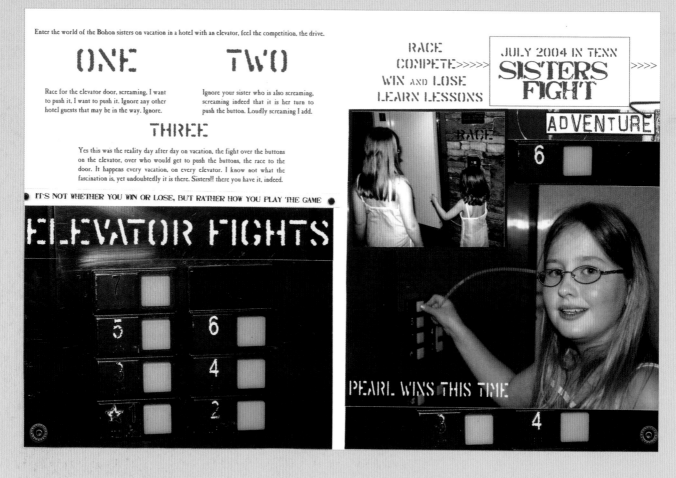

Elevator Fights

vision | Joy wanted to recount the story of her two girls fighting over the elevator buttons.

communication | Notice how Joy created a gathering of text by printing her journaling on the upper left-hand side of her layout. She then repeated this technique with word gatherings on the second page, featuring three distinct blocks of text: one stamped, the other two printed directly onto cardstock.

additional ideas | To balance the large amount of black that the button photo created on the first page, Joy printed an additional photo of the elevator buttons, cut it into strips, and adhered the strips to the second page.

SUPPLIES *Pages by Joy Bohon*
Patterned paper: Rusty Pickle; **Transparency:** 3M; **Rubber stamps:** Limited Edition Rubber Stamps; **Stamping ink:** Memories, Stewart Superior Corporation; **Clip:** 7gypsies; **Brads:** Lost Art Treasures; **Eyelets:** Marcella by Kay; **Computer fonts:** Casablanca Antique, Stamp Act and Trendy University, downloaded from the Internet.

structured text

When creating a gathering of text on your page, consider these options: structure text into a list, place text into boxes, format text into a paragraph or run sentences in vertical or horizontal borders across your page. The possibilities are endless!

Carrie at 27

vision | Carrie wanted to capture her life and personality at age 27.

communication | Carrie chose to keep this layout very simple to keep the focus on the photo. When she saw the photo, the look on her face brought to mind several words that describe where she is in her life. Carrie used a list-style gathering to capture these feelings.

SUPPLIES *Pages by Carrie Colbert*
Patterned paper: KI Memories; **Brads:** Making Memories; **Accents:** K & Company; **Letter stickers:** Liz King, Creative Imaginations; **Computer font:** Unknown, Autumn Leaves.

FIVE WAYS TO GATHER PHOTOGRAPHS ON YOUR LAYOUTS

Although I sometimes like to create layouts that feature just one or two photographs, I also like layouts that include multiple photographs. The challenge in creating a multi-photo layout is often how to place photographs in an eye-appealing way. The following strategies will help you get started.

a photo rectangle

On this layout, I grouped six small photographs to create a rectangular-shaped unit. This strategy is easy to repeat with an even number of photographs.

A Fine Man

vision | I wanted to create a layout around a handwritten letter from my grandfather.

communication | I chose six photos of my grandfather from various times in his life and gathered them together in the top portion of the foundation. Notice how this page is filled with rectangles: the photos, the file folder and the shape of the journaling. Also notice how color is used to unify the design: the black and white slides, the black file folder, and the black-and-white ribbon.

SUPPLIES *Pages by Ali Edwards*
Patterned papers: Daisy D's Paper Co. and Anna Griffin; **Slides:** Narratives, Creative Imaginations; **File folder:** Rusty Pickle; **Ribbon:** Making Memories; **"T" accent:** Nostalgiques, EK Success; **Computer font:** Ghostwriter, downloaded from the Internet.

a photo bar

An easy way to include lots of photographs on one page is to create a photo bar. First, choose your photographs. Next, punch photographs with a square punch. Combine photographs into a long border on your page.

Friends

vision | Celebrate a friendship with a variety of photos from various times and places.

communication | I enlarged one photo as a focal point and added another black-and-white photo on the second page to balance out the first. I chose a background cardstock color that was happy and crisp and simple enough to complement rather than compete with the variety of photos.

additional idea | You can easily print on 12" x 12" paper without having a large-format printer. Simply set up your page for 8½" x 14" (legal paper), type out your journaling, run a test print onto legal paper, and then cut your 12" x 12" paper to 12" x 8½". You can either mount that sheet onto another piece of cardstock or hide the seam with a gathering of photos, a ribbon or another strip of paper.

SUPPLIES *Pages by Ali Edwards*
Textured cardstock: Bazzill Basics Paper; **Acrylic accents:** KI Memories; **Rubber stamps:** Ma Vinci's Reliquary; **Stamping ink:** StazOn, Tsukineko; **Frames:** Making Memories and Scrapworks; **Pen:** Zig Millennium.

a photo montage

A Photo Montage is like a photo bar except the photographs are cut to different sizes and shapes.
Read below to see how Tina created the photo montage on her page.

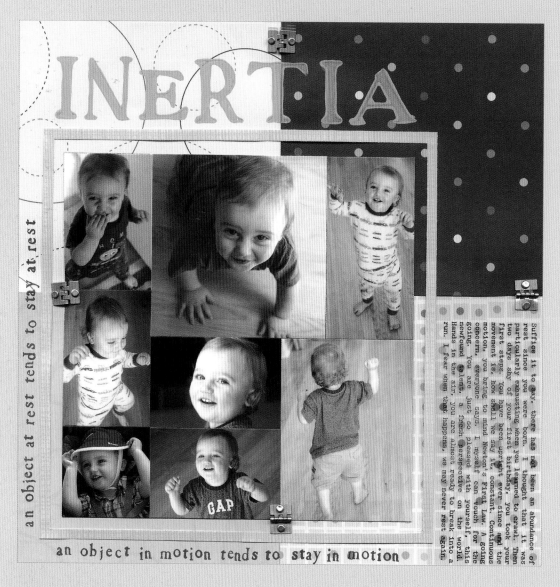

Inertia

vision | Using the concept of inertia, Tina wanted to showcase photos of her son on the move.

communication | On this layout, Tina gathered her photos into an 8" x 8" square. She divided the square into sections manually and then cropped and resized the photos with photo-editing software.

SUPPLIES   *Page by Tina Barriscale*
Patterned papers: KI Memories and Chatterbox; **Transparency:** 3M; **Foam letter stamps, acrylic paint and hinges:** Making Memories; **Small letter stamps:** PSX Design; **Stamping ink:** Ranger Industries; **Computer font:** P22 Typewriter, downloaded from *www.p22.com.*

a photo story

If you have photographs that show a process, you can put them on your page in such a way that they illustrate movement or tell a story. I left space between the photographs to give your mind a chance to process each photograph as a separate part of the story.

Finding your shadow. There it is. There it goes. Here I am. Here I go. You saw your shadow for the first time in March 2004. We all happened to be there. I ran and grabbed the camera and started shooting away. You were giggling and laughing. Investigating. Discovering. It was cool. Love being there when you see something like that for the first time. One of the coolest things about being a parent.

Shadow

vision | I wanted to capture the moment where Simon first discovered and danced with his shadow.

communication | For this page, I placed the photographs of Simon in order, to show him both discovering and dancing with his shadow. I cropped my photos both horizontally and vertically to add additional interest to the page design.

SUPPLIES   *Page by Ali Edwards*
Patterned paper: Chatterbox; **Rubber stamps:** Ma Vinci's Reliquary; **Stamping ink:** ColorBox, Clearsnap; **Circle embellishment:** Nostalgiques, EK Success; **Computer fonts:** ITC Officina Sans, downloaded from the Internet; P22 Cezanne, downloaded from *www.p22.com.*

a photo border

A photo border includes several photographs in a row. Notice that the photographs don't touch (unlike the photographs in a photo bar).

Time to Swim

vision | Joy wanted to capture her daughter doing what she most loved on a family vacation: enjoying the local swimming pool.

communication | Joy wanted to capture the color and the excitement of her daughter's time in the pool, so she chose a color palette that matches Amelia's swimsuit, accented with blue to represent the water. To offset the mats, she gathered patterned papers in a row on the upper-right-hand side of the layout. The variety of patterns helps bring attention to the smaller accent photographs.

SUPPLIES   *Page by Joy Bohon*
Patterned papers: 7gypsies, KI Memories, K & Company and Li'l Davis Designs; **Clips and photo turns:** 7gypsies; **Metal tag:** Making Memories; **Letter stamps:** Limited Edition Rubber Stamps and PSX Design; **Stamping ink:** Tsukineko; Memories, Stewart Superior Corporation; **Woven label:** me & my BIG ideas; **Brads:** Lost Art Treasures; **Computer fonts:** Fake Receipt, GF Ordner Inverted and Blue Highway Type, downloaded from the Internet.

chapter checklist

9 WAYS TO GATHER ELEMENTS ON YOUR LAYOUTS

1. *Use stamped images.*

2. *Use punched shapes.*

3. *Fill metal embellishments such as frames and bookplates.*

4. *Combine different patterned papers using color blocks.*

5. *Group words together to create a meaningful accent.*

6. *Combine fonts and rubber stamps to create a custom look.*

7. *Create a structure in which to place your text.*

8. *Group photographs into a photo bar, border, or montage.*

9. *Choose sequential shots to tell a story.*

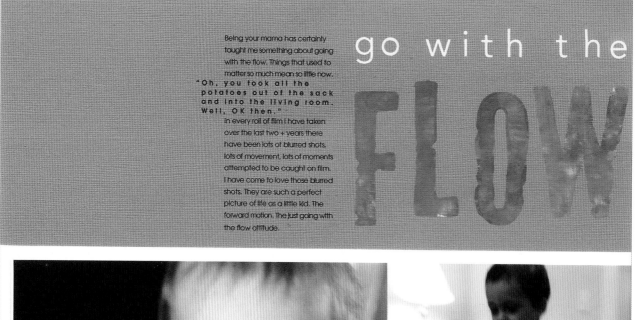

Being your mama has certainly taught me something about going with the flow. Things that used to matter so much mean so little now. "Oh, you took all the potatoes out of the sack and into the living room. Well, OK then." In every roll of film I have taken over the last two + years there have been lots of blurred shots, lots of movement, lots of moments attempted to be caught on film. I have come to love those blurred shots. They are such a perfect picture of life as a little kid. The forward motion. The just going with the flow attitude.

go with the
FLOW

a moment in time

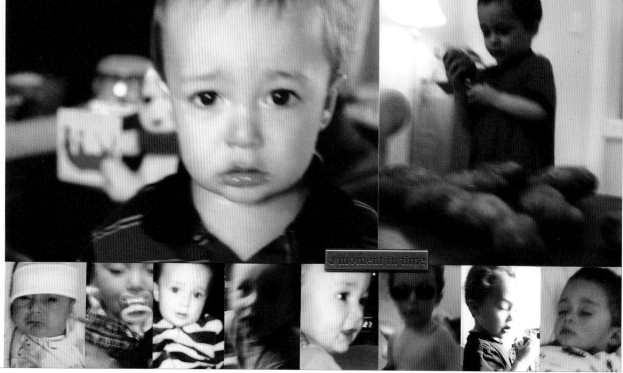

"As hostess (or host), your job is to facilitate the flow. The flow of food. The flow of drink. The flow of conversation. The direction in which the evening should proceed."

— A. Edwards

CHAPTER 4

GO WITH THE *flow*

Facilitating The Flow

When I entertain guests in my home, I always try and plan ahead as much as possible! My goal? To **control** the flow of the evening in a way that's practically unnoticeable to my guests. I want them to feel comfortable, and I want them to come back and visit again.

As a scrapbook designer, I also apply the principle of flow on my scrapbook pages. To create flow on my scrapbook pages, I place my embellishments and photographs in such a way to **lead** my viewer's eye from one element to another. I direct my viewer where to look first, second and third. I want my **viewers** to feel comfortable, and I want them to enjoy looking at my pages. Without flow, a page can be overwhelming and confusing.

When you look at a page with great flow, you see a layout that has a **strong** focal point (often a photo or a title), a nice "line" throughout the page (either literal or implied), and a soft ending point. Flow can be very obvious, such as a line of photos all in a row. Or it can be much more subtle.

In this chapter, I will teach you how to create flow on your pages with paper, embellishments, photographs, and words.

SUPPLIES ON OPPOSITE PAGE   *Page by Ali Edwards*
Textured cardstock: Bazzill Basics Paper; **Foam stamps, rub-ons, metal phrase and acrylic paint:** Making Memories;
Computer font: Avant Garde, downloaded from the Internet.

STRATEGIES FOR CREATING FLOW WITH PATTERNED PAPER

One of the easiest ways to create flow within a layout is to use patterned paper. Striped and/or wavy patterns are an easy way to direct your viewer's eye throughout a page. Look for patterns with strong directional lines when you want to make a statement between elements, and for softer and less obvious lines when you want to simply enhance the movement within a layout.

The Dress

vision | I wanted to celebrate the memories of a friend's wedding.

communication | Notice how the striped patterned paper under the vellum moves the eye from page one to page two. The dominant photos, which face one another rather than off the page, help move your eye across the layout as well.

SUPPLIES   *Pages by Ali Edwards*
Patterned papers: 7gypsies and Autumn Leaves; **Patterned vellum:** Autumn Leaves; **Stickers:** StickyPix; **Label maker:** Dymo; **Rubber stamps:** PSX Design; **Stamping ink:** ClearSnap; **Metal tag and brad:** Making Memories.

FAR LEFT: A pattern with strong directional lines.

LEFT: A pattern with a softer line.

Learning to Fly

vision | I wanted to create a page that shows my husband's love of airplanes.

communication | With the amazing variety of patterned papers available, you never know when you'll come across something that works just right. For this layout, I cropped a sheet of patterned paper with an airplane and placed it in the bottom section of the layout—the direction of the airplane helps the flow move from page one to page two. The lines in the scanned map also add movement to the page; did you notice the line directly between the initial "C" and the title frame?

additional ideas | Create your own patterned paper with material supporting your story. I scanned Chris's flight maps into my computer and printed them on cardstock to use on my layout.

SUPPLIES *Pages by Ali Edwards*
Patterned paper: Autumn Leaves; **Textured cardstock:** Bazzill Basics Paper; **Transparencies:** Narratives, Creative Imaginations; Design Originals (airplane); **Transparency slide:** Paper House Productions; **Definition, pewter frame, brad and phrase:** Making Memories; **"C" sticker:** Pixie Press; **Computer fonts:** Big Caslon and Garamond, downloaded from the Internet; **Other:** Map.

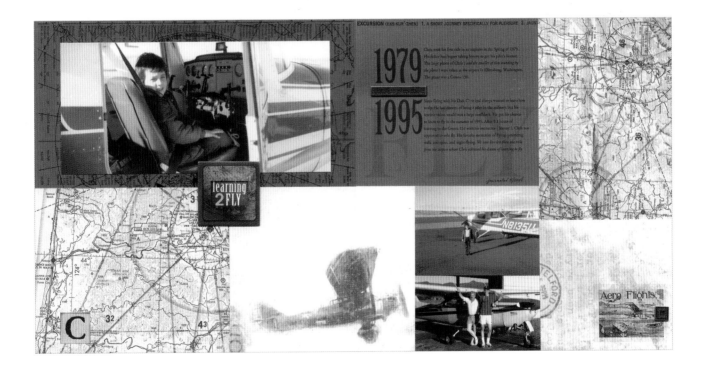

Paper strips are a way to create a literal line across your page. Notice how these lines easily direct your eye across the layout in an effortless way.

This Kid

vision | I wanted to share a sweet story about Simon knocking on our bedroom door in the morning.

communication | Here's an example of a very literal use of line to create flow and contain your viewer within the page. The patterned-paper frame, with one corner removed, specifically directs the viewer from the photo and title into the journaling. An additional flow line is created by the half circle, leading the viewer from the "S" initial to the journaling.

SUPPLIES *Page by Ali Edwards*
Patterned papers: Mustard Moon, 7gypsies and Chatterbox; **Textured cardstock:** Bazzill Basics Paper; **Rubber stamps:** Rubber Stampede, Turtle Press and Ma Vinci's Reliquary; **Stamping ink:** Hero Arts and Clearsnap; **"S" sticker:** Tag Types, EK Success; **Computer font:** 2Peas Hot Chocolate, downloaded from *www.twopeasinabucket.com*.

Christmas 1984

vision | I wanted to create a layout about childhood Christmas traditions.

communication | Notice how the patterned paper along the top, bottom and left side help contain the movement within the page. The three strips of patterned paper on the right balance these elements by not allowing your eye to wander off the page.

SUPPLIES   *Pages by Ali Edwards*
Patterned papers: Daisy D's Paper Co. and Pebbles Inc.; **Rub-ons and square vellum tag:** Making Memories; **Transparencies:** Narratives, Creative Imaginations; **Photo turns:** 7gypsies; **Pen:** American Crafts; **Computer font:** Ghostwriter, downloaded from the Internet; P22 Monet, downloaded from *www.p22.com*.

paper tearing

In addition to straight paper strips, you can also create torn paper strips from patterned paper or cardstock.
Use torn pieces of paper to direct your viewer's eye across your scrapbook page.

50 Years

vision | To showcase a special photo of my grandparents on their anniversary, I
wanted to focus on the number "50."

communication | Drawing your eye toward the photo, the torn paper on this
layout meets at a point almost directly behind the faces of my grandparents. The torn
paper also serves as a nice contrast to the straight lines within the patterned paper.
The clear definitions around the outside of the layout keep your eye within the frame.

SUPPLIES   *Page by Ali Edwards*
Patterned papers: Li'l Davis Designs (numbers), Making Memories (lines); **Textured cardstock:** Bazzill Basics Paper; **Definition,
foam stamp and acrylic paint:** Making Memories; **Round "5":** Provo Craft; **"Remember" sticker:** K & Company; **"Years" and
"M" rub-ons:** Li'l Davis Designs; **Circle tag:** Tag Types, EK Success; **Pen:** American Crafts.

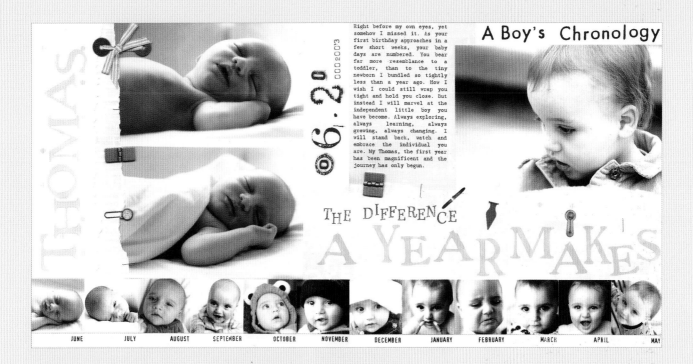

The Difference

vision | Tina wanted to celebrate Thomas's first year of life with a month-by-month timeline.

communication | For this beautiful layout, Tina used paper tearing and embellishments to guide the eye from the name on the first page to the title on the second page. Torn papers on the second page intersect at the corner of the photo. Placing the torn paper directly over the photo creates the impression of a torn photo.

SUPPLIES *Page by Tina Barriscale*
Patterned papers: Creative Imaginations and KI Memories; **Large number stickers:** Creative Imaginations; **Black rub-on letters, foam stamps, acrylic paint, ribbon, staples, brad, photo flips and washer word:** Making Memories; **Black rub-on letters:** Autumn Leaves; **Small letter stamps:** Hero Arts; **Stamping ink:** Memories, Stewart Superior Corporation; **Paper clip:** Nostalgiques, EK Success; **Photo turn:** 7gypsies; **Computer font:** Hartin2, downloaded from the Internet; **Other:** Bookmark.

STRATEGIES FOR CREATING FLOW WITH PHOTOGRAPHS

Did you know that the way you place your photographs on a layout influences the way your viewer "reads" your page layout? In this section, I'll teach you how to direct your viewer's eye across your page through photo placement.

photos: left to right

Your eye naturally "reads" text and photographs from left to right. By placing your photographs in this familiar progression, your viewer will easily follow the elements on your layout.

Hidden Treasure

vision | I wanted to showcase cute photos of a spontaneous Simon "moment" at home.

communication | For this layout, I chose to place the photos from left to right, beginning with the smaller cropped photos and moving toward the large photo on the end. The rounded corners are repeated on the photos, the quote and the journaling block, creating a nice gathering of shapes.

SUPPLIES   *Page by Ali Edwards*
Patterned paper: Cross-My-Heart; **Patterned vellum:** Li'l Davis Designs; **Vellum:** Autumn Leaves; **Corner punch:** Marvy Uchida;
"S" accent: Creative Imaginations; **Stamping ink:** ColorBox, Clearsnap; **Computer fonts:** ITC Officina Sans Book, downloaded
from the Internet; 2Peas Jack Frost, downloaded from *www.twopeasinabucket.com.*

This Is Where

vision | Tina wanted to create a page featuring the landmarks in Saskatoon that were important to her family before they moved from the city.

communication | Tina tightly cropped the landscape photos vertically, gathering them together to lead the eye from left to right across the layout toward the journaling and the second set of photos. The photos in the negative sleeve are also arranged in a logical flow, showing various combinations of family members, ending with a photo of the family together.

additional idea | I loved reading Tina's journaling for this page. She's not just talking about how cool the buildings are—she's using the buildings to speak about her personal growth and her family's growth during their time in Saskatoon.

SUPPLIES   *Pages by Tina Barriscale*
Patterned paper: Mustard Moon; **Transparency:** 3M; **Letter stamps:** Ma Vinci's Reliquary; **Stamping ink:** Brilliance, Tsukineko; **White rub-on dates:** Autumn Leaves; **Rub-on letters:** Making Memories; **Black clips:** 7gypsies; **Negative strip:** Narratives, Creative Imaginations; **Computer fonts:** Love Letter TW and Attic, downloaded from the Internet; **Other:** Saskatoon City street map.

directional photos

Flow can be created by the composition of your photos and the elements within them. Many times there are strong lines in your photographs that you can use to direct flow on your pages.

Time

vision | I wanted to create a page about Simon's personality traits at age two.

communication | When I picked up these photos from the developer, one of the main things I noticed (besides Simon's cute expression) was the strong line created by the car window. Notice how the placement of the square accent on the second page keeps your eye focused on the photo and journaling, without letting you wander up and off the page. In addition, the three accents form a nice visual triangle, repeating the silver frame and color scheme.

SUPPLIES   *Pages by Ali Edwards*
Patterned paper: Scrapbook Wizard; **Textured cardstock:** Bazzill Basics Paper; **Frames:** Making Memories; **Acrylic accents:** KI Memories; **Computer font:** CK Typewriter, "Fresh Fonts" CD, *Creating Keepsakes.*

Find your

[Determination]

At nine, oh you have grown tired-tired of dance, tired of soccer, tired of the girls club. But we want you to be active, we want you to have interests, we want to provide a full and centered life for you. We also want to teach you about the benefits of exercise and maintaining your health. Your father is a black belt in karate-and he thought that would be a perfect fit for you, a sport to pique your interest, and also a way of teaching discipline and focus. So here we are. Practicing front kicks, becoming a bit frustrated at times, not yet feeling the groove, still frustrated with your mistakes. It takes time my dear, time to be good at anything, time and practice and a bit of determination. It is there, behind your public face of frustration, I see that spark and I know you have it in you. Just focus, just breathe, just be and it will fall into place. Spring of 2004

Your inner strength · · · · · · · · Is there I know

[suc·cess]

Determination

vision | Joy wanted to demonstrate her daughter's range of motion as she practiced her karate moves.

communication | Joy communicated her vision for this layout using the stark white of her daughter's karate outfit and the flow of her kick to direct vision from the left to right. She added the large flower on her focal-point photo to grab the eye and lead it to the bottom set of photos. From there, the eye is guided across the page to the other red accent and to the journaling block above. Joy connected the two pages together by adhering a white journaling strip across the pages.

SUPPLIES *Pages by Joy Bohon*
Textured cardstock: Chatterbox and Bazzill Basics Paper; **Flower and frame:** Li'l Davis Designs; **Brads:** Lost Art Treasures; **Rubber stamp:** Making Memories; **Stamping ink:** Memories, Stewart Superior Corporation; **Computer fonts:** Soli and Adjutant-Normal, downloaded from the Internet.

The natural progression of life according to Pearl

Lifelines

vision | Joy wanted to create a page that records her daughter's perspective of growing up.

communication | Take a look at the photographs featured on this layout. Notice the lines created by Pearl's glasses? They help draw your eye across the page. In addition, Joy created flow across both pages through the progression of a timeline along the top and through the labels connecting the two photos together.

additional idea | I love how Joy added color to her layout with the title and journaling—visually the three elements make a nice triangle that moves your eye from one section to another.

SUPPLIES   *Pages by Joy Bohon*
Patterned paper: KI Memories; **Transparencies:** Creative Imaginations; **Label maker:** Dymo; **Number labels:** me & my BIG ideas; **Computer fonts:** Adler, Perpetua and Adjutant Normal, downloaded from the Internet.

STRATEGIES FOR CREATING FLOW WITH EMBELLISHMENTS

With all the embellishments available, we have many options for creating flow on our pages. Embellishments can be lined up or gathered together to move your viewer's eye from one location on your layout to another.

circle-shaped embellishments

Because I'm a very linear scrapbooker, I often reach for circular embellishments to soften and balance my page designs. Look at the following layouts for ways to use circles to facilitate movement on your pages.

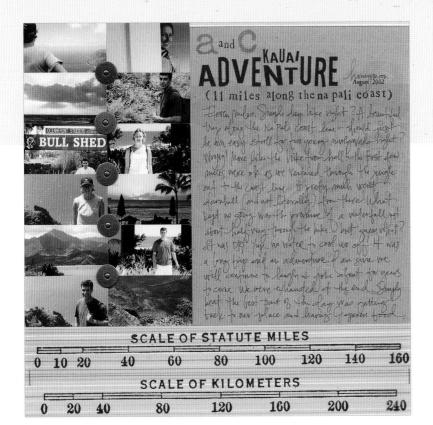

Adventure

vision | I wanted to recount one of the humorous highlights from my honeymoon.

communication | Notice how I placed circular embellishments down the middle of my photo collage. In addition to aiding in the flow, the line of embellishments works to separate and visually differentiate the photos.

additional ideas | Consider scanning images from the Internet that relate to the story you're telling. For this layout, I went online and found a map of the island we visited. To complete the page, I wrote my journaling on top of the scanned map.

SUPPLIES   *Page by Ali Edwards*
Patterned paper: KI Memories; **Transparency:** Narratives, Creative Imaginations; **Map:** Downloaded from *www.bestofhawaii.com*; **Rectangle punch:** Marvy Uchida; **Washers and brads:** Making Memories; **Rubber stamps:** Ma Vinci's Reliquary, Turtle Press and PSX Design; **Stamping ink:** Hero Arts and Ranger Industries; **Date stamp:** Making Memories; **Pen:** Zig Millennium, EK Success.

IT DOESN'T GET MUCH BETTER THAN THIS! IN A CITY KNOWN FOR ITS HORRIBLE TRAFFIC AND LONG COMMUTES, I AM PRIVILEGED TO BE ABLE TO AVOID THAT HUSTLE AND BUSTLE. I AM THANKFUL TO CALL THE WOODLANDS HOME ... HOME FOR BOTH MY HOUSE AND OFFICE! YOU SEE, I LIVE A MERE HALF MILE FROM WORK. MY COMMUTE CONSISTS OF A LEISURELY WALK FROM MY TOWNHOUSE ON THE WATERWAY TO MY SPECTACULAR OFFICE BUILDING ON THE WATERWAY. IT BEATS SITTING IN TRAFFIC ANY DAY! OH HOW I LOVE MY TEN MINUTES OF FRESH AIR AND TIME TO MYSELF EACH MORNING AND EVENING! (MAY 2004)

My Commute

vision | Carrie wanted to tell the story of how the change in her commute has made her life happier.

communication | Carrie achieved flow throughout her layout with the repeated use of circle embellishments. Beginning at the top near her title, the circles lead the eye into the pictures and then on to the journaling.

additional ideas | When selecting colors for this layout, Carrie considered choosing a neutral palette (grays and browns) to emphasize the corporate, professional side to her commute. She realized, though, that her vision was more about how her commute made her life better. With that in mind, she chose bright, cheerful colors and patterns instead.

SUPPLIES   *Pages by Carrie Colbert*
Patterned paper, acrylic accents and die cuts: KI Memories; **Letter stickers:** Wordsworth; **Letter stamps:** Fontwerks; **Stamping ink:** Memories, Stewart Superior Corporation; **Computer font:** 2Peas Tasklist, downloaded from *www.twopeasinabucket.com*.

ribbon

Ribbon is one of the easiest ways to make sure things are flowing in the right direction on your page. As an embellishment, ribbon tends to add structure as well as flow, making it a great choice for an organized layout.

Family Memories

vision | I wanted to celebrate three generations of family together for an afternoon.

communication | On this page, the vertical ribbons draw your eye to the title, the journaling and into the main photo. The punched rectangles in the top create a nice gathering that complements the focal-point photo. When choosing the patterned paper for this page, I loved that this particular paper included that one red circle. It's a nice repetition of the colors found within the shirts in the photographs.

SUPPLIES   *Page by Ali Edwards*
Patterned paper: Autumn Leaves; **Textured cardstock:** Bazzill Basics Paper; **Ribbons:** Li'l Davis Designs and Making Memories; **Rub-ons and antique brads:** Making Memories; **Word stickers:** Bo-Bunny Press; **Rectangle punch:** Marvy Uchida; **Pen:** Pigment Pro, American Crafts.

Scoot in a little closer, kids

Everyone look at me ... hello ... over here

Can we put the bunny ears down please?

Okay then, good enough.

Silliness ruNs In tHe fAmiLY

Silliness

vision | Mellette wanted to capture the fun of a photo shoot.

communication | Mellette used the most intense color of ribbon at the top left of the layout to draw the eye to the top corner. Notice how Mellette chose to place the bottom photo on the opposite side of the tag—this draws your eye over to the focal-point photo.

additional idea | Notice how Mellette's use of the brown papers neutralizes the brighter patterns, ensuring the photos don't become lost on the layout.

SUPPLIES   *Page by Mellette Berezoski*
Patterned papers: The Paper Loft, Bo-Bunny Press, Karen Foster Design and Pebbles Inc.; **Letter rub-ons and eyelets:** Making Memories; **Ribbon:** Making Memories, SEI and C.M. Offray & Son; **Letter stickers:** KI Memories; **Button:** Junkitz; **Computer font:** AL Post Master, package unknown, Autumn Leaves.

stickers

I love how easy it is to use stickers to create flow on my layouts. Think about using stickers that follow a progression such as "1-2-3" or "A-B-C."

The method of operation for you and your Dad regarding play is chase, tickling, wrestling, and making a lot of noise. I am thinking that this must be a common father son thing. I can remember my Dad playing with your Uncle John the same way...and your Dad has told me stories about playing with his Dad the same way too. A guy thing. You are definitely most ready to play this way when Dad comes home - and near bed time. There is always a lot of noise during those times of the day. I watch and smile and head back into my room to escape the shrieks. Inevitably you run into the studio ...and what do I do? Chase you out of course ...adding my own noise to this time of play. Dad laughs. You laugh. I laugh. Another reason why I love our new house - much more room to play and chase and yell and laugh. You are so lucky to have a Dad that loves to play so much -such a kid at heart. April 2004

1, 2, 3 Play

vision | I wanted to showcase the motion of play between father and son.

communication | To emphasize the starting point of my layout, I added a ribbon directing the viewer to the number "1" and placed an "S" initial on this photo. From there the flow moves down the page through the familiar numbers 1, 2 and 3, then to the title, and back up the photos to the journaling. A very subtle arrow in the patterned paper leads you back to the beginning.

SUPPLIES   *Page by Ali Edwards*
Patterned paper: Autumn Leaves; **Letter stickers:** KI Memories; **Date stamp and ribbon:** Making Memories; **Circle letter stamps:** PSX Design; **Stamping ink:** StazOn, Tsukineko; **Computer font:** Gil Sans Light, downloaded from the Internet.

STRATEGIES FOR CREATING FLOW WITH WORDS

The placement of words—and the words themselves—can create flow on your layout. Whether in a straight line, a list or another interesting placement, playing with words on your page and the formatting of their progression can add interest to the design as a whole.

directional text

On the two scrapbook pages that follow, you'll see two examples of how stamped text can be used to facilitate movement across a scrapbook page.

Backyard Life

vision | I wanted to create a layout that showcases the color and life found within our backyard pool.

communication | This layout features words that move up and above the photos, leading the viewer's eye in the general direction of the final block on the second page. Highlighted by larger red stamping, the title of the layout, "Backyard Life," is placed within the flow of words.

SUPPLIES   *Page by Ali Edwards*
Patterned papers: Li'l Davis Designs and KI Memories; **Textured cardstock:** Bazzill Basics Paper; **Stamp stickers:** American Crafts; **Rub-on words:** Li'l Davis Designs; **Beaded flowers:** Beadables, EK Success; **Rubber stamps:** PSX Design and Turtle Press; **Stamping ink:** Tsukineko and Clearsnap.

> **PHOTOGRAPHY TIP**
> Frame your photos in different and unique ways. Get closer. Keep your subject out of the center of the frame. Get even closer.

May 2004

Beautiful Inside

thank you for teaching

me to see myself as beautiful

I was so unique;
now I feel skin deep.
I count on the make-up
to cover it all.
Crying myself to sleep cause
I can't keep their attention.
I thought I could be strong,
but it's killing me.
Does someone hear my cry?
I'm dying for new life.

I want to be beautiful,
Make you stand in awe;
Look inside my heart,
and be amazed.
I want to hear you say who
I am is quite enough;
Just want to be worthy of love
and beautiful.

Sometimes I wish I was someone
other than me.
Fighting to make the
mirror happy.
Trying to find whatever
is missing.
Won't you help me back
to glory?

You make me beautiful
You make me stand in awe
You step inside my heart,
and I am amazed.
I love to hear You say who
I am is quite enough.
You make me worthy of love
and beautiful.

by Bethany Dillon

Beautiful Inside

vision | Carrie wanted to create a layout that celebrates who she is on the inside.

communication | Carrie's layout is a perfect example of using words to move the eye around a design. I love how she began with the vertical cursive title. Her journaling includes song lyrics on the right-hand page and then journaling on strips that guide the eye around the photos.

SUPPLIES *Page by Carrie Colbert*
Patterned paper: KI Memories; **Leather flowers and brads:** Making Memories; **Letter stickers:** K & Company; **Letter stamps:** Hero Arts; **Stamping ink:** Ranger Industries; **Computer font:** Unknown, downloaded from *www.twopeasinabucket.com*.

Don't forget that you can also create flow with your journaling. How you format your journaling—in lines, boxes or paragraphs—can help create flow across your page.

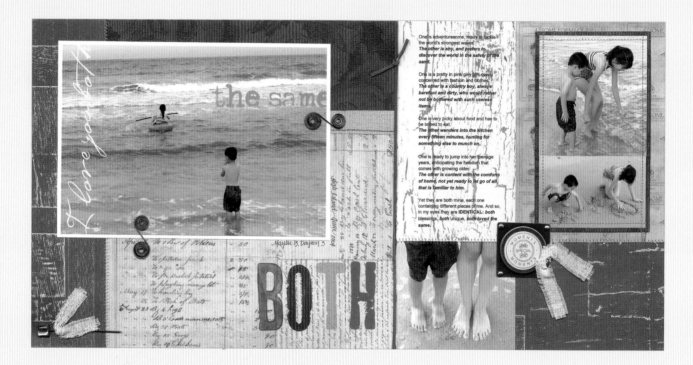

Both

vision | Mellette wanted to celebrate the love she feels for both of her children.

communication | To create flow within her journaling, Mellette repeated words specific to each of her children. The theme (her children's differences) is carried out until the end, when the twist is that they are the same to her. The contrasting idea at the end serves to give the journaling a stopping point or closure.

SUPPLIES   *Pages by Mellette Berezoski*
Patterned papers: The Paper Loft, 7gypsies, K & Company, me & my BIG ideas and Design Originals; **Letter stamps and acrylic paint:** Making Memories; **Metal frame:** Li'l Davis Designs; **Seal:** K & Company; **Pin:** Nostalgiques, EK Success; **Computer fonts:** AL Verdigris and AL Modern Type, packages unknown, Autumn Leaves; Arial, Microsoft Word; **Other:** Leather lacing, fabric and clips.

Wish Upon a Star

vision | I wanted to create a mini book and note holder as a gift for a friend.

communication | One of the things I've found most useful in designing mini books is limiting myself to just a few supplies and then repeating them throughout the book. The result is a cohesive, well-flowing creation.

SUPPLIES   *Book by Ali Edwards*
Patterned papers: Mini Graphics and Autumn Leaves; **Textured cardstock:** Bazzill Basics Paper; **Flowers, pewter accents, mini book and ribbon:** Making Memories; **Stickers:** Brenda Walton, K & Company; **Quotes:** From *Quote Unquote Volume 1*, Autumn Leaves; **Computer fonts:** Calisto MT and P22 Cezanne, downloaded from the Internet.

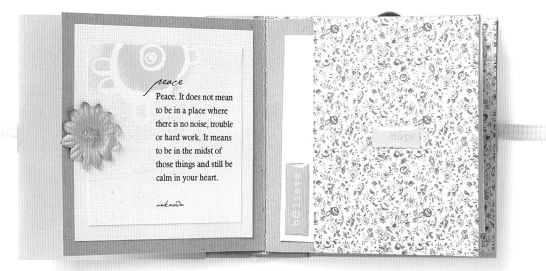

step by step:
"WISH UPON A STAR"

This mini book makes a perfect gift for a new baby, a graduate or a special friend. The interior cards are blank for personalized thoughts and notes.

GATHER:

- 2 sheets of cardstock
- 4 sheets of patterned paper (two each of two patterns)
- Sticker sheet
- Paper flowers
- Metal accents, including brads, photo turns, four washers
- 5 of your favorite quotes
- Computer or journaling pen
- Mini album (I used a Making Memories album)

CREATE:

1. String ribbon through the back of the mini book.

2. Insert the interior pages of the mini book into the cover.

3. Choose which patterned paper you want to use for the quotes and which you want to use as background for the stickers. Print or handwrite the five quotes on your choice of papers. I chose a busier pattern for the stickers.

4. Cut quote squares to 3" x 3".

5. Cut eight 3½" x 3½" squares from cardstock. These will be your interior pieces and the background frames for some of the quotes.

6. Center your printed quotes and adhere.

7. Adhere two washers back to back on the top of two squares and slip inside the pockets with half-moons in the top. Slip the remaining cardstock squares into the pockets and complete with a sticker. These pages are there for you to write a personalized note or add another quote.

8. Cut one 3½" x 3½" piece of patterned paper. Center a quote printed on cardstock and adhere.

9. Cut seven 4" x 4" squares of the busier cardstock. Adhere to pages 3 (trim to fit), 4, 7 (cut out section for half circle), 10 (same as 7), 13 (trim to fit) and 14. Hold onto the square for page 1.

10. Cut two 4" x 4" squares from the patterned paper you printed your quotes on and cut out sections for the half circle. Adhere to pages 8 and 9.

11. For page 1, adhere your title cardstock square to the background patterned paper. Add a small strip of the second patterned paper vertically. Adhere the photo turns with brads and then adhere to the book.

12. Adhere stickers. Adhere flowers with stickers placed in the center throughout, including on the outside of the pocket of the mini book.

Chapter Checklist

4 THINGS TO DO WHEN CREATIVITY ISN'T FLOWING

It happens to all of us—sometimes the ideas just don't flow the way we want them to. The suggestions below will help you get back on track.

take a break. *Stop scrapping. Stop thinking about scrapping (if you can). Do something else for a couple of days. If your ideas start flowing, jot them down in an inspiration journal.*

go shopping. *New supplies can really get me going again if I find myself uninspired. Visit your favorite scrapbook store and look for new items to experiment with.*

scraplift. *Read magazines—and not just scrapbooking magazines. Try art magazines, fashion magazines and photography magazines. One of my favorite things to do is take a trip to Borders and check out their awesome selection of magazines. Taking a break and just browsing through all the eye candy can be so inspirational. Need more ideas? Browse scrapbooking web sites. Online sites offer a wealth of ideas.*

clean out your scrap space. *Re-organize. Purge. Sometimes I do this when I'm trying to save money. As I go through my supplies, I tend to find "treasures" I've forgotten about—these items can inspire me just as much as new ones can.*

"The personality of a house is indefinable, but there never lived a lady of great cultivation and charm whose home, whether a palace, a farm-cottage or a tiny apartment, did not reflect the charm of its owner."

— Emily Post

charm
SCHOOL

The Essence of Charm

As a designer, one of my goals in communicating my vision is to create layouts that are attractive and delightful. I want those viewing my pages to become thoroughly involved, to lose themselves in the story, to be captivated by the photos, engaged in the details. I want my viewers to be *charmed* by my layouts.

Charm can be created through thoughtful consideration or through spontaneous intuition. Sometimes it's a bit of both. Often, charm is *developed* by taking cues from the decisions you've already made in the process of designing your page. The photos you chose may contain a color that will make a wonderfully *attractive* coordinating embellishment or work perfectly as a background foundation. Your journaling may include a word, or evoke a feeling, that can be capitalized on for a *striking* title or cool typographic accent. Your goal is simply to create a page that is delightfully irresistible.

In this chapter, I'll teach you how to invoke charm through the use of color, photographs and words.

SUPPLIES ON OPPOSITE PAGE   *Page by Ali Edwards*
Patterned papers: Mustard Moon, The Paper Loft, 7gypsies, Daisy D's Paper Co., Scenic Route Paper Co., Chatterbox, Anna Griffin and Design Originals; **Transparency:** Daisy D's Paper Co.; **Patterned vellum:** SEI; **Decorative-edged scissors:** Fiskars; **Square punch:** Marvy Uchida; **Acrylic paint and large letter stamps:** Making Memories; **Small letter stamps:** PSX Design; **Rectangle stamp:** Technique Tuesday; **Stamping ink:** Ranger Industries; **Numbers:** Li'l Davis Designs; **Rub-on:** Autumn Leaves.

INVOKING CHARM THROUGH COLOR

One of the easiest ways to infuse charm into your pages is to make good use of color. Color is a powerful generator of charm. Taking some time to assess how color makes you feel can go a long way in enabling you to create pages that leverage the full potential of color.

bold colors

Look for bold colors in your photographs that you can use to grab your viewer's attention.

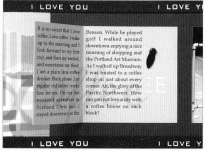

Coffee

vision | I wanted to create a page from photos of all the coffee shops I came across one morning in downtown Portland.

communication | Taking cues from the photos, I incorporated the color orange as a main element in my design. The "A" calls attention to itself through the contrast with the beige cardstock, yet it also acts as a unifier within the design by repeating the orange found in the photos.

SUPPLIES *Page by Ali Edwards*
Patterned paper: Mustard Moon; **Patterned vellum:** KI Memories; **Letter stamps, acrylic paint, ribbon, rub-ons, brad and photo turn:** Making Memories; **Coffee cup dingbat:** 2Peas David Walker Dingbats, downloaded from *www.twopeasinabucket.com;* **Computer font:** Palatino, downloaded from the Internet.

contrasting colors
Try mixing a bold color with a contrasting color in a soft or muted tone.

Sprinkler

vision | I wanted to create a layout that showcases Simon's joy of playing in the sprinkler.

communication | Contrasting the bright-red paper with the muted background elements sets apart the entire red section as my focal point. The white type on the red stands out and draws your eye into the design.

SUPPLIES *Pages by Ali Edwards*
Patterned papers: KI Memories, Chatterbox and Anna Griffin; **Patterned vellum:** American Crafts; **Transparency:** Creative Imaginations; **Textured cardstock:** Bazzill Basics Paper; **Rub-ons:** Autumn Leaves; **Hinges:** Making Memories.

seasonal colors

What colors do you associate with each season? Use those colors to create a charming look and feel on your seasonal scrapbook pages.

Signs of Summer

vision | Mellette wanted to capture the signs her family associates with summer.

communication | Mellette chose solid cardstock rather than patterned paper to help keep the focus on the photos. Notice the great use of shape on this page: Mellette created a gathering of circles, including the main journaling circle located on the top photo. The buttons on the title, as well as the round colored brads on the photo anchors, also echo the circle theme.

SUPPLIES *Pages by Mellette Berezoski*
Textured cardstock: Bazzill Basics Paper; **Vellum:** Paper Adventures; **Letter rub-ons:** Scrapworks; **Buttons:** Junkitz; **Ribbon charm and metal number charms:** Making Memories; **Epoxy letter sticker:** Creative Imaginations; **Computer font:** Broadcast, downloaded from the Internet.

soft colors

When choosing colors for your page, consider the mood you want to evoke. Soft colors give your page a different look and feel than bold or bright colors.

Grandparents

vision | Mellette wanted to celebrate the love and devotion her parents have for their grandchildren.

communication | According to Mellette, "I saw so much love and devotion in these pictures, I wanted to create a layout that really let the photos speak for themselves." She chose a soft color palette to help emphasize the warmth evoked in the photos.

additional idea | Mellette has a fantastic knack for pairing patterned papers to evoke moods on her pages. For this layout, she combined five different patterns.

SUPPLIES   *Page by Mellette Berezoski*
Patterned papers: me & my BIG ideas, Anna Griffin, K & Company and 7gypsies; **Woven label and jump ring:** Junkitz; **Circular frame:** Pebbles Inc.; **Woven photo corners and paper flowers:** Making Memories; **Letter sticker:** K & Company; **Round medallion:** EK Success; **Computer font:** AL Post Master, package unknown, Autumn Leaves; **Other:** Ribbon.

favorite colors

Quick, what's your favorite color? Think about incorporating shades of your favorite color into your pages about yourself.

Pictures of Happiness

vision | Carrie wanted to link special photos of her and her sister to the things in life that make her happy.

communication | To balance Carrie's bold use of colors, patterns and textures on this layout, she chose a simple white background as her foundation. When attempting a page with a bold use of color, don't be afraid to experiment with combining patterns from different companies or even different styles of paper.

SUPPLIES *Pages by Carrie Colbert*
Patterned papers: KI Memories, Doodlebug Design and Creative Imaginations; **Handmade paper:** The Jennifer Collection, Sakar; **Bookplate:** Creative Imaginations; **Stickers:** American Crafts ("Happy"), Creative Imaginations ("Sisters"); **Acrylic accents and die cut:** KI Memories; **Title rub-ons:** KI Memories ("Picture of"), Scrapworks ("Happiness"); **Computer fonts:** Steelfish Outline, downloaded from the Internet; AL Remington, package unknown, Autumn Leaves.

> **JOURNALING TIP**
> Remember, just a small change of the text color from black to other colors can make a big difference in the overall communication of your page.

retro colors

When scrapbooking photographs from earlier decades, consider using colors that were popular at the time. You'll often find these colors reflected in your photographs.

John

vision | I wanted to create a page detailing a single day in my brother's life.

communication | The red line, the "Joy" woven label, the red stamping and the red in the Superman shirt all come together, creating a nice bit of charm and making the layout feel connected and complete.

additional idea | I'm so blessed to have so many photos to "play" with from my childhood. Is there a budding scrapbooker in your family who may love to play with your photos someday down the road? Consider organizing all your duplicate photos and jotting down a bit of information on the backs.

> **DESIGN TIP**
> White next to any saturated color tends to highlight whatever is placed on or in the white foundation.

SUPPLIES   *Page by Ali Edwards*
Patterned paper: Mustard Moon; **Textured cardstock:** Bazzill Basics Paper; **Vellum:** Autumn Leaves; **"Joy" woven label:** me & my BIG ideas; **Black rectangle** *accent:* KI Memories; **Brads:** Two Peas in a Bucket; **"J" stickers:** American Crafts and The Paper Loft; **Airplane sticker:** Pebbles Inc.; **Airplane card:** me & my BIG ideas; **Definitions, acrylic paint and "J" sticker:** Making Memories; **Pens:** Staedtler (red); Zig Millennium, EK Success; **Letter stamps:** PSX Design; **Stamping ink:** ColorBox, Clearsnap.

INVOKING CHARM THROUGH PHOTOS

Photos are inherently charming. We look for similarities and connections. We look for a glimpse into the lives of other people. Photos speak directly to the viewer.

personality photographs

Do you have a favorite photograph of yourself? Is it a reflection of who you are? Does it capture your true personality? The pages showcased in this section include photographs that are inherently charming in the way they capture each subject's personality.

Dad & Mom

vision | I wanted to create a page that discusses how I wish I could have known my parents when they were just beginning their lives together.

communication | Using Adobe Photoshop, I scanned, enlarged and adjusted this photo to a duotone (one color and black). I created a small patterned-paper frame to single out my parents and then repeated that rectangle shape with a title also created in Photoshop (printed at the same time I printed the photo).

SUPPLIES *Page by Ali Edwards*
Patterned papers: Daisy D's Paper Co. and Scrapbook Wizard; **Circle stickers:** Sonnets, Creative Imaginations.

Bliss

vision | When I saw this photograph, I knew that one big smile simply deserves one big word!

communication | Every now and then, there's a photo that just needs to be cropped tightly and enlarged for maximum impact. The large, red "Bliss" calls attention to itself, repeating a word found in the quote from Mother Theresa. The large photo is balanced out by the stamped word (and the color red), making it a bit less top-heavy than if it were created without the large word.

SUPPLIES *Page by Ali Edwards*
Textured cardstock: Bazzill Basics Paper; **Definition stickers:** Pebbles Inc.; **Rubber stamps:** Ma Vinci's Reliquary; **Stamping ink:** ColorBox, Clearsnap; **Computer font:** Ghostwriter, downloaded from the Internet.

The Ground Beneath Her Feet

SUSAN COOPER
SUMMER 1947

A small child, playing in the sand on the British seaside nearly sixty years ago. She bears a striking resemblance to the child I was three decades ago and to my own three year old son today. Over the years I have forged a greater understanding of my own mother, where she came from, her life experience. As the three year old in the photograph gazing upon the vast ocean, I wonder if she ever imaged some twenty years later she would indeed cross the great Atlantic. Not to visit, but to live, sight unseen in a remote town in the corner of north-western Canada, at a mere twenty-three years of age. She left behind family, friends, and the only country she had ever known, for a life of adventure and opportunity. And here I sit today, her Canadian daughter, so very thankful that her mother took that risk.

SCALE OF KILOMETERS

0   20   40   80   120   160   200   24

It is good to have an end to journey towards but it is the journey that matters in the end

Beneath Her Feet

vision | Tina wanted to create a special layout that focuses on this photograph of her mother as a small child.

communication | For this layout, Tina chose a photo of her mother that bears a strong resemblance to Tina as a child, and to her son as well. The transparencies (the title, journaling and scale) build upon the theme of the page, assist in the flow and work to keep your eye within the layout. For an even more historic look, Tina painted and sanded the molding strips, mitered the corners, and used them to frame two edges of the page.

additional idea | Tina chose to use the title of a book which was a favorite of both hers and her mothers, a collection of children's books titled *The Faraway Tree Series* by Enid Blyton.

SUPPLIES   *Page by Tina Barriscale*
Patterned paper: Li'l Davis Designs; **Transparencies:** Narratives, Creative Imaginations; 3M; **Molding strips, paper flowers and acrylic paint:** Making Memories; **Canvas tag:** Creative Imaginations; **Clips:** 7gypsies; **Rub-ons:** Autumn Leaves; **Computer fonts:** P22 Cezanne, downloaded from *www.p22.com*; American Typewriter Light, downloaded from the Internet; **Other:** Brads.

This is Liz. Today she is a scientist. A
scientist who studies wood and wood
scientist
products and so much more than I will
ever know about. Not too many women
smart
in her profession. She is so smart.
Looking at her here it is easy for me
to imagine how she got to where she
is today. She is ambitious. She has
drive. And she is very much a lady.
entertainer
She is a fabulous entertainer. A
creative
fantastic cook. A super creative
decorator. I just love visiting her and
seeing what she has been up to.
Liz is my sister-in-law. My brother is
so lucky. And I am so lucky that she is
a part of my life. I can not wait for
Simon to have some cousins!

Liz

vision | I wanted to create a layout that showcases my sister-in-law's personality.

communication | On this layout, the photos express personality. They are the charm of the page. The strong vertical lines form a barrier with the photos, but Liz's expression in the main photo leads you back across the strips and into the journaling. The small initial accent also helps break up the hardness of the black lines.

SUPPLIES   *Page by Ali Edwards*
Patterned papers: KI Memories and Scrapworks; **Textured cardstock:** Bazzill Basics Paper; **Flower brads:** Making Memories; **"L" accent:** Li'l Davis Designs; **Computer fonts:** P22 Monet, downloaded from *www.p22.com*; Georgia, Microsoft Word.

methods and manners

Scrapbooking is so much about making connections, and about bringing those connections and shared experiences to life in our scrapbooks.

"day in the life" photographs

What do you see outside your window each day? What's your child's daily routine? Photographs that capture your everyday experiences can be full of charming stories that are perfect for your pages.

Irene

vision | I wanted to share the story of my parent's neighbor, Irene.

communication | The photo that shows Irene in action, doing what she has done every day for the last 10 years, is the main source of charm for me on this layout. The photo of Irene feeding the gulls is the view my parents have through a window in their kitchen. It's as much a part of their lives as it is Irene's.

additional ideas | I created the layered look on this layout by lining up three patterned papers and covering them with vellum. Using a craft knife, I cut a rectangle about ¼" larger than the photo. This allows the background cardstock to peek through, providing a nice frame for the photo.

SUPPLIES *Pages by Ali Edwards*
Patterned papers: K & Company, Mustard Moon, Scrapbook Wizard and me & my BIG ideas; **Textured cardstock:** Bazzill Basics Paper; **Patterned vellum:** Autumn Leaves; **Transparency:** Narratives, Creative Imaginations; **Ribbon, pewter word phrase and date stamp:** Making Memories; **Letters and circle holders:** Li'l Davis Designs; **Computer font:** Palatino, downloaded from the Internet.

artistic photographs

As a scrapbooker, I'm always taking pictures—of everything! I sometimes capture an "artistic" photograph of an inanimate object. Your "artistic" photographs may have a charm of their own that you want to include on a scrapbook page.

Create Art

vision | Inspired by the perspective (and color) of these inanimate photos, Joy wanted to capture an art-filled experience.

communication | The line of brads on the left-hand side help with flow and are attached to a strip cut from the large photo at the right to help with color coordination. The label and the clips further help in leading the eye throughout the design. The textual elements are arranged in a visual triangle on the right-hand page.

SUPPLIES   *Pages by Joy Bohon*
Rubber stamps: Limited Edition Rubber Stamps ("Imagination"), Stampers Anonymous ("Create"); **Stamping ink:** StazOn, Tsukineko; **Bookplate:** Magic Scraps; **Epoxy word and sticker:** Wordz, Creative Imaginations; **Clips:** 7gypsies; **Brads:** Lost Art Treasures; **Label maker:** Dymo; **Computer fonts:** Casablanca Antique and Ticket Capitals, downloaded from the Internet.

INVOKING CHARM THROUGH WORDS

I love playing with words and using different sizes and shapes of type (fonts, handwriting, and alphabet stickers, rub-ons, and rubber stamps are all examples of type) to enhance my page layouts. I like to think about type in terms of loud and quiet. In some cases, I want the type to scream. Large stamps or fonts are a great way to incorporate loud type into your layouts. In other instances, I want the type to be as unobtrusive and quiet as possible. To achieve this, I use the same font at a small point size or even hide the journaling altogether. The decision should be made based on the vision you're attempting to communicate. In this section, I share layouts that incorporate different types of type.

loud type

Loud type makes a bold statement on your page. Here are three scrapbook pages that show you how to incorporate loud type into your layouts.

You and Him

vision | I wanted to celebrate the relationship between my husband and our son.

communication | The type on this layout is layered—similar to the layering of Simon and Chris in the photos (you see more of Simon in the photos than you see of Chris). Noticing little details like this helps create harmony on the page.

SUPPLIES ON OPPOSITE PAGE *Page by Ali Edwards*
Patterned papers: Chatterbox, K & Company and The Paper Loft; **Frame:** Li'l Davis Designs; **Letter stamps:** Ma Vinci's Reliquary and PSX Design; **Stamping ink:** Ranger Industries and Hero Arts; **Pen:** Zig Millennium, EK Success.

The Age of Email

vision | I wanted to design a page celebrating the impact e-mail has had on my life.

communication | In Adobe Photoshop, I created a 12" x 12" canvas that included the enlarged "@" and a portion of an e-mail I had received (which was simply copied and pasted and repeated in a variety of sizes). I then printed the image on a transparency, cut it in half, and adhered it to each page of the layout.

SUPPLIES *Pages by Ali Edwards*
Patterned paper: KI Memories; **Textured cardstock:** Bazzill Basics Paper; **Cardstock tag and hemp fabric:** Artistic Scrapper, Creative Imaginations; **"E" stamp and acrylic paint:** Making Memories; **"@" stamp:** Stampers Anonymous; **Letter stamps:** PSX Design; **Stamping ink:** StazOn, Tsukineko; **Transparency:** Artistic Expressions; **Charm:** Wood Life, Creative Imaginations; **Stickers:** Memories Complete; **Brads:** Two Peas in a Bucket; **Computer font:** Myriad, Microsoft Word.

Only 33

vision | Joy wanted to create a page that reflects on her life as it is today, at age 33.

communication | Joy designed a bold, charm-filled title for this page that immediately catches your attention. It makes a statement. Joy chose tightly cropped black-and-white photos of herself, reinforcing the words in her journaling: a sense of being overwhelmed, sometimes boxed-in, fragile. The starkness of the layout allows the focus to be on the title, the photos and the words.

SUPPLIES   *Page by Joy Bohon*
Bottle caps: Li'l Davis Designs; **Label maker:** Dymo; **Computer fonts:** GF Ordner Inverted, Bell MT and 20,000 Dollar Bail, downloaded from the Internet.

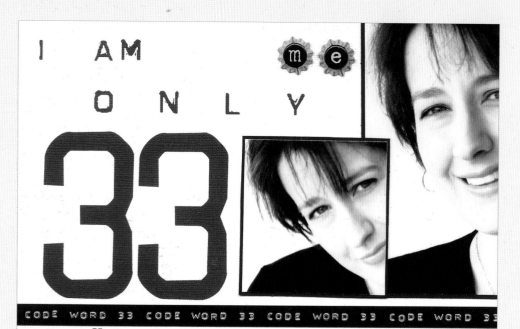

I am only 33—Ah not perhaps that many would think that is young…but it is more than that. This little phrase…It has become a code word between my husband and I, a phrase that I utter when I am completely and irrevocably overwhelmed, overwhelmed with life, overwhelmed with motherhood, overwhelmed with my career, just generally one woman pulled a hundred different directions on a daily basis. These little words, they let me express my fragility, my sense of drowning in a world that sometimes moves all too fast for me. Yes , I am 33- I am a wife, the mother to precocious little girls, the homemaker, the family planner, the shopper, the maid, the bill payer, and I am also a physician to thousands. My days are not my own, my plans are often swept awry by the needs of others, by the call of labor, by the urgency of a sick child, or at times by someone who just needs to talk, just needs me to hold a hand and to feel their loss. And I do not easily let go, I bring these problems home heavy on my heart, oh so many days. Some days I can only take baby steps, some days I feel I stride boldly, some days are hard, some days are easy, and I never know which they shall be.

Sadness and joy, they fill my working days. Up and down from one room to the next as I see my patients, the mood different with each door I open, sometimes I see tears and sometimes I see contentment, always I see someone that I can try to help. It matters not at the time that I am 33, I do what I need to do, what I am trained to do, and what I have learned to do, I do not think of age or even of my own vulnerability in a time of need-but then in the silence of the night, re-living the day, I feel sometimes that overwhelming sense of need from everyone and everything that surrounds me, and sorrow for the sadness in life that I cannot change, and then I say to my husband, my soulmate, my confidant, the one who has been there with me since the beginning of all of this.. I say ..but I am only 33

CODE WORD THIRTY THREE
33

quiet type

Quiet type can make a subtle statement on your page. Notice how the journaling on these two pages takes up a relatively large amount of space on each page. Because I've used quiet type, the journaling doesn't overwhelm my other page elements.

Percolate

vision | I wanted to create a page about my studio space.

communication | Not just "My Studio," but "My Little Castle" (and in French, no less). And not just "the place where my ideas come together," but where they "percolate." Play with words. Have fun focusing on the words you're choosing for your page.

SUPPLIES   *Page by Ali Edwards*
Fabric paper: me & my BIG ideas; **Vellum:** Autumn Leaves; **Slide holders:** Narratives, Creative Imaginations; **Rubber stamp:** Ma Vinci's Reliquary; **Stamping ink:** ColorBox Fluid Chalk, Clearsnap; **Brad:** Making Memories; **Computer font:** 2Peas Hot Chocolate, downloaded from *www.twopeasinabucket.com*; **Other:** Fabric.

A Perfect Day

vision | I wanted to recount a summer day with friends while reflecting on our relationship.

communication | This layout is obviously about the journaling. It takes up quite a bit of space on the page. It's quiet in the sense that it's not shouting to be noticed, but it's powerful and calls attention to itself simply by its size. Notice the subtle elements of three: the red in both of the children's shirts combines with the ribbon and the stamping. The light blue of the library pockets and the strip of patterned paper along the bottom unify the colors within the design.

SUPPLIES *Page by Ali Edwards*
Patterned papers: Anna Griffin and Chatterbox; **White tag and ribbon:** Making Memories; **Library pockets:** Li'l Davis Designs; **Silver rectangle charm:** K & Company; **Rubber stamps:** Technique Tuesday; **Stamping ink:** Ranger Industries; **Brads:** Two Peas in a Bucket; **Word stickers:** Bo-Bunny Press; **Computer font:** Modern No. 20, downloaded from the Internet.

mixed type

I like to mix and match type sizes and styles to create a custom look on my layouts.

bigwheels

Boys and their bikes. One of your Dad's favorite memories is when he got this big wheel. I am sure it is a story you will be hearing a lot in the years to come. He loved that big wheel. Loved to race it around. Loved the feeling of "driving." You were pretty excited to see this big wheel in our bedroom on Christmas morning 2003. You looked surprised - then trotted right over and jumped right on. Ready to ride. You have not gotten the hang of peddling yet - but you like to sit on the seat and drive yourself around with your legs. Good exercise for your legs for sure! I am looking forward to the day that it all comes together for you - when it makes sense that you peddle to get yourself going. Then you can zoom all around the back patio and the driveway - what a feeling of freedom. Just like your Dad.

Big Wheels

vision | I wanted to compare photographs of my husband and son with their first "Big Wheels."

communication | Creating charm with type contrast is easily achieved by placing thick and thin typefaces next to one another. Changing the color of one adds even more dynamic interest.

SUPPLIES   *Page by Ali Edwards*
Patterned paper and vellum: American Crafts; **Textured cardstock:** Bazzill Basics Paper; **Stickers:** Mrs. Grossman's ("C" and "S"), Bo-Bunny Press (white stickers); **Computer fonts:** Arial Bold and Helvetica, Microsoft Word.

Boys and cars. The love affair has now officially commenced here at the Edwards! Simon is all about attempting to get up into the front seat each time we go out to the car now. Let him get up there once and he was IN LOVE with all the buttons and the steering wheel and the gear shifts and the radio and on and on and on. And, well, it's only 14 years until he gets his license...

Car

vision | I wanted to document Simon's love of car keys and his love of sitting in the front seat of our car.

communication | On this layout, I also used mixed type. Notice how I combined two different type styles on this page: my handwritten journaling AND a border strip (and accent piece) taken from a piece of alphabet patterned paper. The letter "C" at the top of my journaling box helps direct your eye to the story I share on this page.

SUPPLIES *Page by Ali Edwards*
Patterned papers: Chatterbox (stripe), K & Company (car) and source unknown (letters); **Vellum:** EK Success; **Textured card-stock:** Bazzill Basics Paper; **Key and typewriter key:** DMD, Inc.; **Ribbon:** Making Memories; **Rectangle punch and corner rounder:** Marvy Uchida; **Other:** Tags.

chapter checklist

7 WAYS TO ADD CHARM TO YOUR LAYOUTS

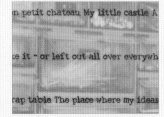

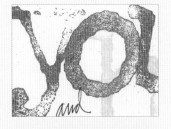

1. *Use colors that support the mood and theme of your layout.*

2. *Choose your photos to reflect your subject's personality.*

3. *Create a layout using "everyday" photographs.*

4. *Try your hand at taking "artistic" photographs to support the theme of your layout.*

5. *Use "loud" type to make a bold statement on your layout.*

6. *Use "quiet" type to make a subtle statement on your layout.*

7. *Mix up your type styles to create a custom look.*

The ultimate quest. finding balance. learning balance. learning to share to give and to take. You and Ruby... you were so shy. Hiding with your eyes closed until you warmed up. And then learning to share toys and

S & R

GIVE
AND
TAKE

later lives. Finding balance... and yourself.

MAY 2004

"Good conversation is all about give and take — Excel at each."
—Kate Spade

give AND TAKE

Creating the Perfect Balance

Give and take is an important part of conversation—and of life! I know that I'm continually striving to achieve a comfortable *balance* in my life between my family and my work. It can be such a challenge! I add time for one activity, take time away from another, reschedule and *schedule* again—such is life. Balance sometimes seems so elusive, yet I've discovered that if I take time to slow down and focus on what's most important that I can bring myself back to a happy sense of calm stability.

Balance is also an important *element* of scrapbook page design. As I create pages, I'm constantly striving for balance within my design. I make decisions as I create. I move elements from one place to another. I add. I subtract. I *give*, and I *take*. Balance on a scrapbook page is about creating a harmonious and well-designed layout that effectively communicates your vision.

In this chapter, I will teach you five different ways (and numerous variations!) to achieve balance on your scrapbook pages.

SUPPLIES   *Page by Ali Edwards*
Patterned vellum: SEI; **Textured cardstock:** Bazzill Basics Paper; **Foam stamps and acrylic paint:** Making Memories; **Rub-ons and accent tabs:** Autumn Leaves; **Stitched stickers:** K & Company; **Pen:** American Crafts.

50/50 BALANCE

A simple way to create balance on your pages is to create a layout consisting of half text and half photographs. Here are three different ways to place your photographs and text in a harmonious way.

vertical columns

Pretend like your page is divided into two vertical columns. Fill half the space with journaling and the other half with photographs.

Moving On, Growing Up

vision | I wanted to tell the story of the decision to have Simon attend preschool earlier than I had expected.

communication | This page is balanced by the use of two vertical rectangles (one words, the other photos) and a foundation that is off center. The off-center foundation gives additional weight to the journaling side by visually enlarging the area.

SUPPLIES *Page by Ali Edwards*
Patterned paper: Daisy D's Paper Co.; **Letter stickers:** Colorbök; **Mini tag:** Making Memories; **Zipper pull:** All My Memories; **Rubber stamp:** PSX Design; **Stamping ink:** ColorBox Fluid Chalk, Clearsnap; **Brad:** Two Peas in a Bucket; **Computer font:** Baskerville, downloaded from the Internet.

horizontal columns

Imagine that your page is divided into two horizontal columns. Fill one column with journaling and the other column with photographs.

Growth

vision | I wanted to create a page that compared two photographs of myself (and I wanted to journal about my emotional and physical growth).

communication | To emphasize the differences in myself from one time to another, I chose patterned papers that fit with my personality during each time period. Notice how I placed my photographs in the upper half of the page and my journaling in the lower half of the page.

SUPPLIES   *Page by Ali Edwards*
Patterned papers: me & my BIG ideas, Rusty Pickle and Scrapbook Wizard; **Vellum:** Autumn Leaves; **Transparency:** Magic Scraps; **Accent:** The Card Connection; **Rubber stamp:** Ma Vinci's Reliquary; **Stamping ink:** Hero Arts; **Computer font:** ITC Galliard, downloaded from the Internet.

split columns

You can split your photographs and text across two columns—and across two pages of a layout.

Approach to the Park World

vision | Joy wanted to tell the story of an ordinary day that became magical.

communication | In this example, Joy created a half text/half photo layout where each individual page represents roughly half of the space. Notice how she didn't make the text areas the same size as the photo sections. Rather, Joy decided to use the text space on the first page for an expanded title.

SUPPLIES *Page by Joy Bohon*
Metal hangers: Jest Charming; **Brads:** Making Memories; **Computer fonts:** Hootie, BlueCake, Times New Roman and Casablanca Antique, downloaded from the Internet.

BIG/LITTLE BALANCE

A large photograph (or grouping of photographs) placed next to or across from a small photo can create balance within a layout. Here are two layouts to show how to use big/little balance on both a single and double page spread.

Generations

vision | I wanted to create a page that focuses on the generational love between fathers and sons.

communication | With a small color photo contrasted by a large black-and-white photo, this page achieves a strong sense of balance. Overlapping the photos results in a direct connection, showcasing the relationship between the two.

SUPPLIES   *Page by Ali Edwards*
Patterned papers: K & Company and KI Memories; **Textured cardstock:** Bazzill Basics Paper; **Transparency:** K & Company; **Letter stickers:** Doodlebug Design and Scrapworks; **Ribbon:** Making Memories; **Clock rubber stamp:** Rubber Stampede; **Stamping ink:** Hero Arts; **Mini folders:** DMD, Inc.; **Poemstone:** Creative Imaginations; **Pen:** Zig Millennium, EK Success; **Computer fonts:** American Typewriter, downloaded from the Internet; P22 Cezanne, downloaded from *www.p22.com*.

Characteristically You

vision | Inspired by photos of Simon's organizational characteristics, I wanted to design a page that discusses his personality and documents this day in time.

communication | One of my favorite ways to communicate a story on a layout is to showcase one photo on the first page and a gathering of photos on the second page. The contrast between the two is an easy way to create balance across a two-page spread.

SUPPLIES   *Pages by Ali Edwards*
Patterned papers: Anna Griffin and Creative Imaginations; **Textured cardstock:** Bazzill Basics Paper; **Patterned vellum:** KI Memories; **Ribbon and "S" accent:** Li'l Davis Designs; **Circle accents:** KI Memories; **Circle punch:** Punch Bunch; **Computer font:** Eurostyle, downloaded from the Internet.

> ### JOURNALING TIP
> Take time to write about what makes your subject unique and endearing.

MIRRORED BALANCE

One way to achieve a balanced look on your page is to create a layout where one side of the page reflects the other side of the page. Mirrored balance can be achieved in different ways. In this section, I present four different ways to achieve this type of balance on your page.

direct reflection

In this type of balance, one side (or half) of the layout is a direct reflection of the other side.

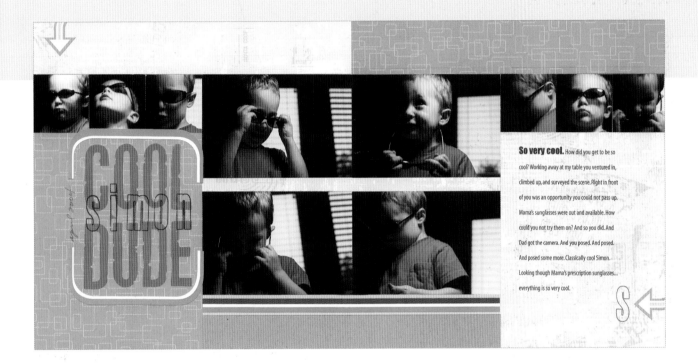

Cool Dude

vision | I wanted to create a page that captures the coolness of Simon as demonstrated in these photos.

communication | In this example, the right-hand side of the layout is a direct reflection of the left hand side of the layout. I added elements that appear visually equal on each page (the title and the journaling block), with added emphasis on the title.

additional idea | Taking a large number of photos gives me several options when it comes to creating scrapbook pages.

SUPPLIES   *Pages by Ali Edwards*
Patterned papers: KI Memories and Creative Imaginations; **Textured cardstock:** Bazzill Basics Paper; **Rubber stamps:** Fontwerks and Making Memories; **Stamping ink:** StazOn, Tsukineko; **Stickers:** Sassafras Lass; **Computer font:** Myriad Condensed, Microsoft Word.

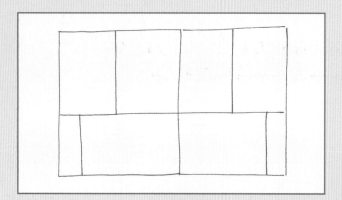

It Must Be a Sign

vision | Carrie wanted to capture the fun memory of staying at a hotel in Paris with her last name: the Hotel Colbert. Says Carrie, "This was definitely a unique situation that needed to be documented!"

communication | Notice how Carrie's title fills one section of the left-hand side of her layout, while the mirror opposite section is filled with journaling.

SUPPLIES *Pages by Carrie Colbert*
Patterned paper: KI Memories; **Letter stamps:** PSX Design and Fontwerks; **Stamping ink:** Memories, Stewart Superior Corporation; **Ribbon:** Scrap Wizard; **Letter stickers:** K & Company; **Brads:** Making Memories; **Computer font:** Various fonts from Autumn Leaves and Two Peas in a Bucket.

quarter turn

In this second type of mirrored balance, the elements on the right-hand side of the layout have been rotated 90 degrees clockwise from the elements on the left-hand side of the layout.

Playing

vision | I wanted to create a page highlighting Simon's current favorite playthings.

communication | Do you see how I rotated the design of the second page? Notice how my title section and my journaling section become mirror reflections of each other in terms of page space.

SUPPLIES   *Pages by Ali Edwards*
Patterned paper: Kangaroo & Joey; **Rubber stamps:** Stampabilities (letters), PSX Design (circles); **Stamping ink:** Colorbox, Clearsnap; **Circle accents:** KI Memories; **Circle frames:** Scrapworks; **Circle letter stickers:** EK Success; **Computer fonts:** ITC Officina Serif, downloaded from the Internet; Apple LiGothic, package unknown.

upside down

Start with your original elements and turn them "upside down" on the second half of your layout. Take a look at these layouts (and my sketches) to see three different ways to apply this technique to your scrapbook pages.

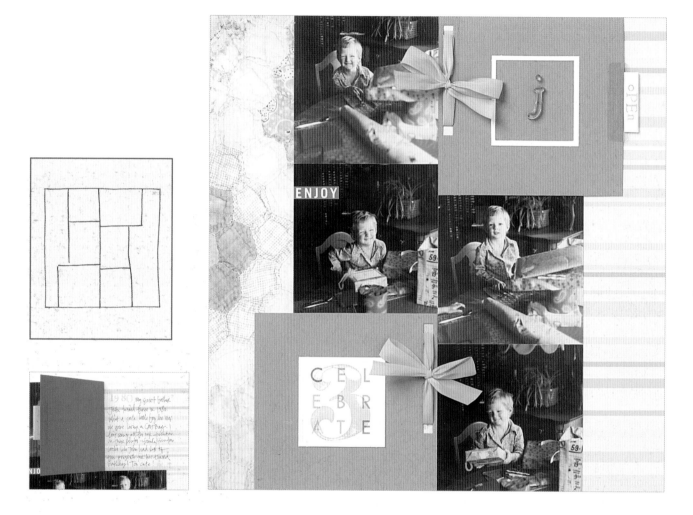

Celebrate 3

vision | I wanted to construct a page that celebrates my brother's third birthday.

communication | The patterned papers on each side balance each other well because they're essentially the same colors. The elements on the right-hand side of my layout are positioned "upside down" from the elements on the left-hand side of my layout.

additional ideas | The top square card opens to reveal hidden journaling.

SUPPLIES   *Page by Ali Edwards*
Patterned papers: Doodlebug Design and me & my BIG ideas; **Square accent and "J" accent:** KI Memories; **"Enjoy" sticker:** Making Memories; **Rubber stamps:** Ma Vinci's Reliquary (large "3"), PSX Design ("Open" and "1980"); **Stamping ink:** ColorBox Fluid Chalk, Clearsnap; **Ribbon:** Florilegium; **Label:** Staples; **Chipboard:** 7gypsies; **Pen:** Zig Millennium, EK Success.

Picture Yourself

vision | Tina wanted to create a layout that documents William's affection for trains.

communication | Take a look at the two sides of this layout. Do you see how the design of the second page is, well, simply turned upside down? The only difference is that the large block on the first page is comprised of two photos (whereas the second is one enlarged photo).

SUPPLIES *Pages by Tina Barriscale*
Patterned papers: Chatterbox, KI Memories and SEI; **Rub-ons and leather frames:** Making Memories; **Label maker:** Dymo; **Stamping ink:** Memories, Stewart Superior Corporation; **Bookplates and acrylic accents:** KI Memories; **Twist ties:** Pebbles Inc.; **Computer font:** 2Peas Chestnuts, downloaded from *www.twopeasinabucket.com*.

Athlete in Training

vision | Mellette wanted to capture the many moves of her budding athlete.

communication | Mellette created this very cool layout by using the principle of "upside down" balance. The elements on her first page are rotated 180 degrees to create the second page. The group of small photos on the first page contrasts with the large single photo on the second page.

additional ideas | Mellette inked the red embroidered "B" to give it an aged look and to tone down the brightness. She also soaked the white shoelaces in walnut ink for a more worn appearance.

SUPPLIES *Pages by Mellette Berezoski*
Patterned papers: The Paper Loft, K & Company and Mustard Moon; **Transparency:** Creative Imaginations; **Definition and soccer ball stickers:** Karen Foster Design; **Vintage sports stickers:** Sticker Studio; **Tacks and eyelets:** Chatterbox; **Antique clip:** EK Success; **Label maker:** Dymo; **Number sticker:** Li'l Davis Designs; **Computer font:** Adler, downloaded from the Internet; **Other:** Embroidered letter and shoelaces.

Zoo Tag Book

vision | I wanted to create a tag book that teaches Simon about the animals at the Oregon Zoo.

communication | The simple repetition of elements combined with a basic page design makes this book a good example of effective balance. I formatted and printed information about each animal directly onto patterned paper that I then trimmed to fit the size of the book.

additional idea | Make the most of what you have! After having our zoo photos developed, I was treated to several blurry photos. Rather than be upset, I decided to use those photos anyway. The blurriness evokes a ton of emotion.

SUPPLIES   *Book by Ali Edwards*
Patterned paper: The Paper Loft; **Tag book and pins:** 7gypsies; **Black square initials:** Li'l Davis Designs; **Butterfly stamp:** Paper Angel; **Stamping ink:** StazOn, Tsukineko; **Bookplate:** KI Memories; **Ribbon:** May Arts; **Computer font:** Myriad, Microsoft Word; **Other:** Twine.

BEYOND THIS PAGE: *mini book balance*

For this mini book, I created a very basic page style and followed it throughout the book; the result is a well-balanced design. A title, text and accent on one side is complemented and balanced by a photo on the second page. Don't make design more complicated than it has to be—focus on the vision and what you want to communicate and simply build from there.

asian elephant

How does an elephant use its trunk?
The elephant's trunk is unlike anything else in nature. In addition to using it to gather food, breathe air, suck water, and lift, pull, or drag objects, an elephant also relies on its trunk for its strong sensitivity to smells.

How do elephants keep cool?
Elephants keep cool by wallowing in mud; the mud that's trapped in the folds of an elephant's skin stays moist after the elephant has finished wallowing, and as the moisture evaporates, the elephant is cooled. An elephant can also keep cool by flapping its ears; the flapping of these paper-thin body parts helps to cool the elephant's blood as it passes through them, and then the cooled blood travels to other body parts.

hippo
[hippopotamus amphibius]

Home: Rivers, lakes, swamps, and wallows of Africa

Description: Barrel-shaped, blue-gray body with pink belly, large head, stumpy legs.

The Hippopotamus, whose name means "river horse", is a plant-eating water-loving giant. A relative of camels, pigs, and deer, the hippo has two lives in one! The center of a hippo's day life is water. Like a hippo pool-party, sometimes hundreds of hippos, will share a territory of water during the day. Whether it's mating, playing, fighting or giving birth, hippo's all wet. The hippo's night life begins a few hours after sunset, when all the hippos file out of the water to graze on land by the light of the moon.

[unknown] FISH

Your Dad and I tried to figure out what kind of fish this is - but we have no idea! What I did find online is that there are three classifications of fish: **[1] Class Agnatha** (jawless fish) - these primitive fish have no jaws, do not have paired fins, and have a skeleton made of cartilage (not bone). Examples: hagfish, lampreys. **[2] Class Chondrichthyes** (cartilaginous fish) - these fish have a skeleton made of cartilage, paired fins, and no swim bladder. Their skin has tooth-like scales (called denticles). Fertilization of eggs is internal. Examples: sharks, skates, rays. **[3] Class Osteichyes** (bony fish) - these fish have a skeleton made of bone and paired fins. They also have teeth that are fixed onto the upper jaw. Bony fish do not have to swim to breathe.

sun BEAR

The sun bear has a short, sleek, black coat. The muzzle is short, and gray to faint orange in color. The crescent-shaped chest patch is yellowish or white. The muzzle is shorter and lighter colored than that of a black bear and in most cases the white area extends above the eyes. The ears are small and round. The paws are large and the soles are naked, which is thought to be an adaptation for **climbing trees**. The claws are large, curved, and pointed. **This is the smallest of the bears**. Adults are about 120 to 150 centimeters (48 to 60 inches) long and weigh 27 to 65 kilograms (60 to 145 pounds). Sun bears are **omnivorous**. They live in lowland **tropical rainforests**. They are excellent climbers and are thought to sleep in trees.

SUN BEAR

Out in the Open

vision | Carrie wanted to create a page that serves as an illustrated journal of self-discovery.

communication | While a scrapbook may not be the best place to discuss in detail the trials of life, a scrapbook layout is a perfect place to journal about how these trials have made you a better person, about how these hard times have grown your faith and much more. Notice Carrie mentioned specific life trials (divorce, abuse, depression), but she did not focus on that. The focus is clearly on how she overcame and how she has grown.

SUPPLIES *Page by Carrie Colbert*
Patterned paper and die cut: KI Memories; **Letter stamps:** Ma Vinci's Reliquary; **Letter stickers:** me & my BIG ideas; **Date stamp:** Making Memories; **Computer font:** Cecilia Roman, downloaded from the Internet; **Other:** Stamping ink.

WHITE SPACE BALANCE

When I create a layout, I'm always thinking about the principle of "give and take." Sometimes, I'll create a layout and simply "give" too much—too many embellishments or photographs, perhaps. At that point, when my layout feels out of balance, I'll "take" away a few things to make my layout work. When you create a layout, you can create balance by leaving space on your layouts. Here are two examples to show you how to effectively use white (or empty) space on your layout.

Easter 2004

vision | I wanted to construct a page that celebrates Simon's first egg hunt.

communication | I gave a lot to the first page. It's covered with photos. In order to create balance between the two pages, I designed a second page that gives the viewer a chance to rest. I linked the pages together by repeating the small tags and flowers. Notice that I chose a photo for the center of the first page that has a bit of breathing room built into it. The cement in the background gives the eye a resting spot in the middle of the collage of photos.

SUPPLIES *Page by Ali Edwards*
Textured cardstock: Bazzill Basics Paper and KI Memories; **Window tags:** KI Memories; **Labels, rub-ons and brown tags:** Autumn Leaves; **Flowers:** Making Memories; **Computer font:** AL Highlight, package unknown, Autumn Leaves.

Finding Your Style

vision | Joy wanted to capture the essence of her daughter, Pearl, in all her color.

communication | Joy placed the large photo askew on the green mat, lending the majority of weight to the second page. She arranged the other elements in columns around the main photo to balance the design.

additional ideas | Joy let the green of the mat show through the metal frames. This is such a cool way to break up that space and bring the green and the white together.

SUPPLIES *Page by Joy Bohon*
Metal bookplate and keyhole: Li'l Davis Designs; **Ribbon:** 7gypsies; **Transparency:** 3M; **Woven label:** me & my BIG ideas; **Computer fonts:** Mechanical Fun and Casablanca Antique, downloaded from the Internet.

YOU came back from your float trip in tie dye heaven. You and the older girls there had a blast dying shirts and bandannas, and you find the bandanna itself an easy coverup for your summer hair. It hides the wind blown look, keeps the hot sun off your head and keeps mom from noticing the little tangles. I have to smile at you, I have to be thankful that I have a daughter who can light up the day with her bright colors and easy smile. I see you experiment with new things, see you open your eyes to fashion and style and creativity and see you find what suits you the best. Your individuality and personality shine so brightly. I see it here in this photo, topped off with that bright little bandanna, and I am so thankful that I have you frozen in time, just for a moment, in my camera lens. Pearl Danae Rachelle age ten. 06/2004

FINDING YOUR STYLE

TEN

TRENDY

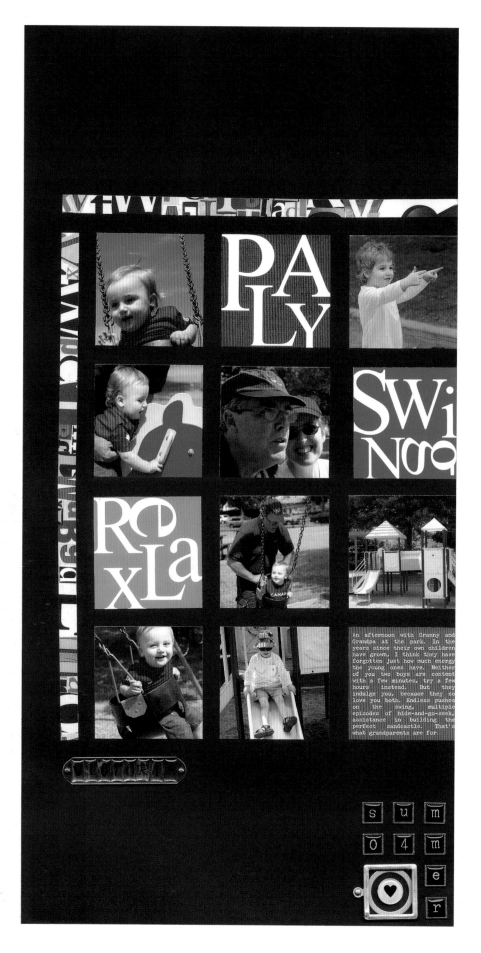

Play, Swing, Relax

vision | Tina wanted to design a page featuring a gathering of squares that incorporates bright and colorful park photos.

communication | Black cardstock makes a dramatic statement and reinforces the concept of "white" space very effectively on this layout. Tina positioned the gathering of photos to the left and vertically off center to create additional interest.

additional idea | Go vertical! Try something new by creating a vertical 12" x 12" double-page spread. This shift from a horizontal to a vertical orientation may really stretch your creative muscles.

SUPPLIES *Pages by Tina Barriscale*
Patterned paper: Rusty Pickle; **Heart accent:** KI Memories; **Silver frame:** Pebbles Inc.; **Letter frames, epoxy letters and numbers, and bookplate:** Li'l Davis Designs; **Computer font:** P22 Typewriter, downloaded from the Internet.

methods and manners

Journaling Give & Take: Life is a fine line between give and take. I know I'm always searching for that delicate balance, walking the tightrope as a wife, mother, artist and woman. As scrapbookers, our goal is to record our stories through photos and words and art. I believe that our scrapbook pages should reflect that give and take within our own lives—the good and the bad, the easy and the hard, the ups and the downs.

Scrapbooking about challenges we face will shed light on our lives for future generations. Letting our children know truths about ourselves (when the time is right) can be educational, enlightening and give them the sense that they're not alone as they become parents, professionals and adults. Your words don't have to be profound; what's most important is that they are your words.

There's no reason to tell your deepest darkest secrets, unless that's your desire. Simply acknowledging within your scrapbook that life is filled with struggles and challenges will make you even more real to those you love and to those you'll never know. Looking back at photos I have of my family from the early 1900s fills me with wonder—wonder about the people. What were their lives really like? What were their struggles? What brought them joy and passion? Those are the things I wish I knew, and those are the things I plan to tell ... in addition to the celebrations and vacations and simple everyday events in our home.

OFF-CENTER BALANCE

When you think about creating a balanced page, remember that you don't have to line everything up perfectly. In fact, you can create eye-catching page designs by deliberately placing your page elements off-center. You'll see examples of how this works in the next two layouts.

Amazing

vision | I wanted to create a page that contrasts similar photos of Simon and me.

communication | Another way to design a well-balanced layout is to create a "page within a page" that's skewed off center to one side or another. For this layout, I developed a vertical background, with the patterned paper taking up about two-thirds of the 12" x 12" space. By placing the rectangle of informational elements off center toward the smaller section of the foundation, the page becomes balanced.

SUPPLIES *Page by Ali Edwards*
Patterned papers: SEI and 7gypsies; **Circle accents:** SEI; **Letter stamps:** PSX Design; **Stamping ink:** Ranger Industries and Hero Arts; **Stickers:** Pebbles Inc.

chapter checklist

6 WAYS TO DECIDE WHAT TO GIVE AND TAKE ON YOUR LAYOUTS

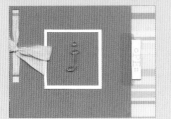

1. *Divide your layout into vertical columns.*

2. *Divide your layout into horizontal columns.*

3. *Use a combination of big and little photographs next to each other.*

4. *Create a mirror image on your page layout.*

5. *Create balance by using mirrored images in which one side of the page layout has been rotated.*

6. *If you want to journal about the balances in your life, feel free to share only as much as you want to share—hide the rest of the journaling.*

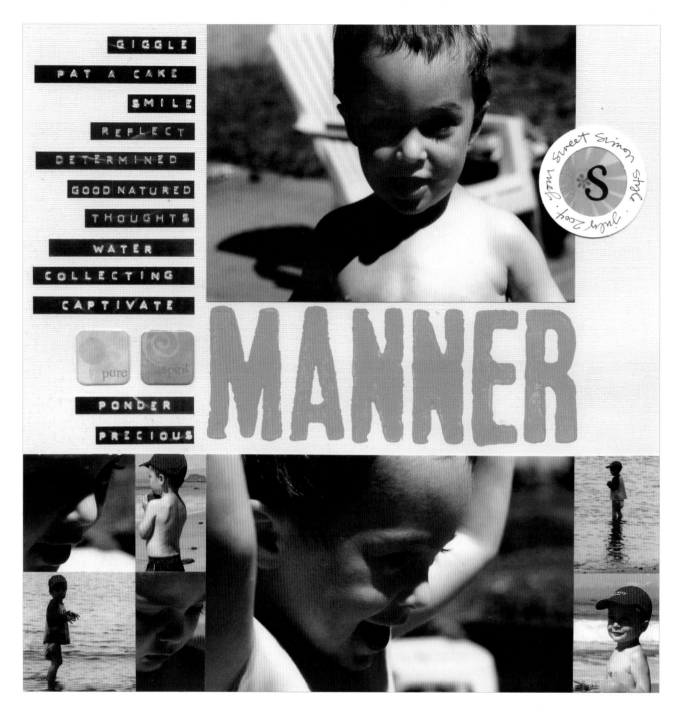

GIGGLE
PAT A CAKE
SMILE
REFLECT
DETERMINED
GOOD NATURED
THOUGHTS
WATER
COLLECTING
CAPTIVATE

pure   spirit

PONDER
PRECIOUS

MANNER

sweet Simon style · July 2004

"... it would have lacked something, somewhere, if you added nothing of your own personality to its perfection."
— Emily Post

CHAPTER 7

MIND YOUR

Manners

Your Own Sense of Style

One of the things I love most about scrapbooking is that it's a direct **reflection** of me. Through my pages, I can add a bit of myself, my personality, my style, to the record of my life and the lives of my family. As a professional designer, most of the time I'm bound to restrictions based on the needs of my clients, but when I'm my own client, the sky's the limit.

Each one of us has an individual style. In the first chapter, I explained that you are indeed a visionary. Part of being a visionary is harnessing your individual experience, embracing your personal style and using that to create meaningful scrapbook pages. Your manner is simply the way in which you translate your personality into your layouts. Adding your own personality, and truly embracing your own style, is at the heart of creating scrapbook pages that best communicate your vision.

This chapter is all about identifying and creating your own style. To help you get started, I've analyzed my own style (as well as the styles of scrapbook designers Tina, Mellette, Joy and Carrie). In addition, I'll help you answer the question, "what's my style?"

SUPPLIES ON OPPOSITE PAGE *Page by Ali Edwards*
Textured cardstock: Bazzill Basics Paper; **Patterned fabric:** Michael Miller Memories; **Square and "S" accents:** Sonnets, Creative Imaginations; **Label stickers:** Pebbles Inc.; **Circle accent:** KI Memories; **Foam stamps and acrylic paint:** Making Memories.

MY STYLE

My creative manner consists of the things I love and continually seem to repeat on my pages. Here is an analysis of both my design and journaling.

MY DESIGN MANNER

use of space

When I create a page, I begin with a piece of cardstock. As I build my foundation, I make decisions about whether my foundation will include that sheet of cardstock or be covered with patterned paper or other elements, or a combination of both. In general, I love to have most elements (photos, journaling blocks, etc.) touching the edge of the paper and one another within the composition.

Edwards' Home

SUPPLIES *Page by Ali Edwards*
Textured cardstock: Bazzill Basics Paper; **Hemp paper and negative holder:** Creative Imaginations; **Frame:** Li'l Davis Designs;
Nailhead and photo turns: 7gypsies; **Brads:** Two Peas in a Bucket; **Computer fonts:** P22 Arts and Crafts and P22 Monet,
downloaded from *www.p22.com*.

horizontal orientations

I love using horizontal layout foundations (across the page), especially on two-page spreads. It's pleasing to my eye, to my sense of give and take, and tends to be the initial way I set up my pages when I begin the process of design.

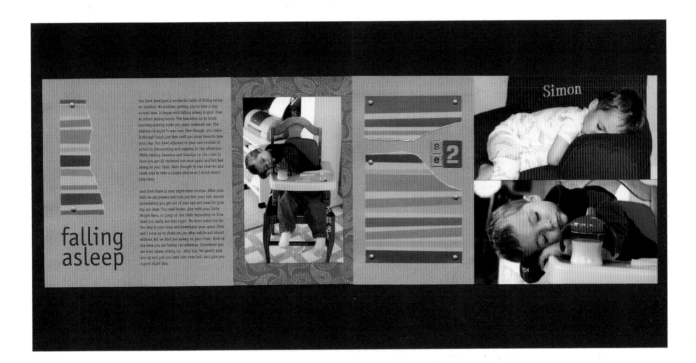

Falling Asleep

SUPPLIES   *Pages by Ali Edwards*
Patterned paper: Chatterbox; **Patterned vellum:** American Crafts; **Letter and number accents:** Li'l Davis Designs; **Brads:** Making Memories; **Computer fonts:** ITC Officina Sans and ITC Officina Serif, downloaded from the Internet.

lined-up elements

I love to work with basic shapes, such as squares and rectangles. A simple way to incorporate these shapes into a space is to line them up vertically or horizontally. An organized line-up of elements is very visually appealing to me.

Chris' 6th Birthday

SUPPLIES   *Pages by Ali Edwards*

Patterned papers: Making Memories and KI Memories; **Textured cardstock:** Bazzill Basics Paper; **Die cut:** Making Memories; **Letter stickers:** Chatterbox; **Word stickers:** Bo-Bunny Press; **Rubber stamps:** Ma Vinci's Reliquary ("C" and "6"), Stamps by Judith (square), Scrap Goods (circle), Making Memories ("Chris"); **Stamping ink:** ColorBox Fluid Chalk, Clearsnap.

layering

Even if you consider yourself a simple scrapbooker, you can make effective use of layers to communicate your vision. Layer papers. Layer embellishments. Even layer photos.

Time for Fish

SUPPLIES *Pages by Ali Edwards*
Patterned papers: KI Memories (orange flower), K & Company (ruler) and Karen Foster Design (fish); **Patterned vellum:** Design Originals; **Letter stickers:** Chatterbox; **Stamp punch:** McGill; **Pen:** American Crafts; **Ribbon:** May Arts; **Clocks:** Li'l Davis Designs; **Brads:** Making Memories.

combination of technology and traditional paper-crafting

As a graphic designer, I get to combine my love of technology and my love of hands-on creativity. The same is true for each of us as scrapbookers. The computer is a great tool that allows me to manipulate my photos or journaling in ways that simply wouldn't be possible without technology.

This Is Me

SUPPLIES   *Page by Ali Edwards Inspired by Barbara Carroll*
Patterned paper and transparency: K & Company; **Textured cardstock:** Bazzill Basics Paper; **Circle and "A" rub-ons:** Creative Imaginations; **"Reflection" sticker:** Pebbles Inc.; **Brads and word rub-ons:** Making Memories; **"Time" sticker:** Li'l Davis Designs; **Transparent "A":** Carolee's Creations; **Pen:** Zig Millennium, EK Success.

MY JOURNALING STYLE

real language

In general, I try to use the same type of language on my layouts that I use in my everyday speech. I call Simon "dude," I pause for emphasis, and often times I simply write out the thoughts that are in my head. I'm also fond of using notes and letters from family members, celebrating their language and personality within my pages.

From: Pati
Date: Tue Dec 23, 2003 1:36:54 PM US/Pacific
To: Ali
Subject: Merry Christmas-2003

Hi Simon,

Over the hills and through the woods to Simon's new house do we go. As we travel along we reminisce of the wonderful times celebrating the Birth of Christ with family and friends. Each of these celebrations represents the growth of ourselves and of our families with God's love responsible for all that we are. To you, Simon, we bring our love and our prayers that your life experiences will bring you happiness and a strong value of faith and trust in God and family.

We will see you soon!
Departing 1:40 PM December 23, 2003

Grandma Pati and Grandpa Al

remember No. 1

{First christmas in our new house}

Merry Christmas

No. 1 Christmas

SUPPLIES   *Page by Ali Edwards*
Patterned paper: The Scrapbook Wizard; **Transparencies:** Narratives, Creative Imaginations; Artistic Expressions; **Rubber stamps:** Ma Vinci's Reliquary; **Stamping ink:** ColorBox Fluid Chalk, Clearsnap; **Woven label:** me & my BIG ideas; **Computer font:** Hoefler Text, downloaded from *www.twopeasinabucket.com*; **Other:** Brads.

reflection

My journaling tends to focus on my thoughts and feelings rather than restating the facts of an event. There's a place in my scrapbooks for both. But the kind I love, that has really become a part of my creative manner, is more reflective than fact by fact.

Seasons

SUPPLIES *Page by Ali Edwards*
Patterned paper: K & Company; **Textured cardstock:** Bazzill Basics Paper; **Vellum and stamp stickers:** American Crafts; **Rub-on letters and brads:** Making Memories; **Rubber stamps:** Stamps by Judith; **Stamping ink:** Hero Arts; **Pen:** Zig Millennium, EK Success; **Other:** Twill.

connections

I love to make connections between past and present, old and new on my pages. I'm always looking for patterns in our lives (and in my photos) that can become topics for layouts.

Flowers

SUPPLIES *Pages by Ali Edwards*
Transparency: Narratives, Creative Imaginations; **Textured cardstock:** Bazzill Basics Paper; **Circle and rounded corner accents:** KI Memories; **Pen:** American Crafts; **Letter stamps and acrylic paint:** Making Memories; **Letter stickers:** Chatterbox; **Other:** Staples.

humor

Thank you, God, for humor. I like my pages to have a sense of humor. For me, it's therapeutic to laugh at myself, at the antics of Simon (and Chris), and at the silly things that happen in our lives.

Happy Hangers

SUPPLIES   *Page by Ali Edwards*
Patterned cardstock: The Paper Loft; **Textured cardstock:** Bazzill Basics Paper; **Rubber stamps:** Turtle Press and PSX Design;
Stamping ink: ColorBox Fluid Chalk, Clearsnap; **Safety pins, flower brad and paper flowers:** Making Memories; **Charm:** All My
Memories; **Pen:** Pigma Micron, Sakura; **Other:** Fabric.

real life

The good and bad. My pages are a give and take of my positive and negative experiences.
I want people to know that my life was filled with both, and that it was okay with me
because it was mine. It gives my life personality and character and always makes me
thankful for the things that are wonderful.

High School Me

SUPPLIES *Page by Ali Edwards*
Patterned papers: 7gypsies, KI Memories, The Paper Loft and K & Company; **Transparency:** Narratives, Creative Imaginations;
Washers: Nostalgiques, EK Success; **Rub-ons and metal frame:** Making Memories; **Letter stamps:** PSX Design; **Stamping ink:**
StazOn, Tsukineko; **Square punch:** Marvy Uchida; **Pen:** Zig Millennium, EK Success; **Other:** Ribbon.

Two Little Boys

SUPPLIES   *Pages by Tina Barriscale*
Patterned papers: KI Memories (green), Li'l Davis Designs (text) and Mustard Moon (striped); **Label maker:** Dymo; **Letter stamps:** It's My Type and Ma Vinci's Reliquary; **Acrylic paint, metal "&" and hinge:** Making Memories; **Wooden number tiles:** Li'l Davis Designs; **Metal letter clips:** Scrapworks; **Tacks:** Chatterbox; **Computer font:** Warnock Pro Light Subhead, downloaded from the Internet.

Just Along for the Ride

SUPPLIES   *Pages by Tina Barriscale*
Patterned paper and acrylic accents: KI Memories; **Definitions:** Making Memories; **Colored rub-ons:** Scrapworks; **Date rub-ons:** Autumn Leaves; **Letters:** Li'l Davis Designs; **Metal frames:** Li'l Davis Designs and Scrapworks; **Computer font:** Nicotine Stains, downloaded from the Internet.

tina's manner

1. **REFLECTIONS OF TIME.** Tina often combines photos from different times and places into one complete layout.

2. **GATHERINGS OF EMBELLISHMENTS AND PHOTOS.** Tina has a wonderful gift for bringing together both embellishments and photos into her layouts. She uses series of photos that add depth to her stories and added embellishments that ground her designs.

3. **NEUTRALITY.** Using a neutral background allows Tina's foundations and overall design to come more from the placement of photos and embellishments than the paper itself.

4. **HUMOR.** Tina says, "I try to incorporate humor into my layouts while telling my stories. When you have small children, the topics can be fairly mundane, so I like to put an interesting twist on them."

5. **FULL USE OF SPACE.** Notice how Tina fills the space on her layouts with journaling and photographs, bringing her elements to the very edge of the page.

6. **MISMATCHING.** "I always like to use something on my page that doesn't quite match," says Tina. "I really like the dissonance and interest it creates. I did this with the blue and brown ribbon on 'Just Along for the Ride.' The brown and the gray are a little off together, but I like it. Generally I don't ever worry about getting exact matches."

7. **CONNECTED ELEMENTS.** Tina loves using elements that connect one area of the design to the next. An example of this is the hinge she used to connect the journaling to the rest of the page on "Two Little Boys."

8. **EMBRACING IMPERFECTION.** "One thing that's a constant in my work is that I'm imperfect," says Tina. "I don't measure out each element within my design, I just eyeball. Things rarely match up exactly; I like a bit of a mess. If you notice the title on 'Two Little Boys,' the stamping with acrylic paint is far from perfect. There are smudges, off spacing and overlapping into the next section. But I like that, and it's part of my style. I want my pages to focus on the photographs and the journaling. I strive to create pages with creative design and use of embellishments that enhance the vision."

Favorite Things

SUPPLIES *Page by Mellette Berezoski*
Patterned papers: Deluxe Designs, Chatterbox, Mustard Moon, The Scrapbook Wizard, K & Company and Creative Imaginations;
Patterned vellum and slide mount: Color Oasis, EK Success; **Letter stamps, acrylic paint, vellum tag, labels, hinges, stick pin,**
decorative stamp, metal letter charm and ribbon: Making Memories; **Flower charm:** Hirschberg Schutz & Co.; **Jump rings:**
Junkitz; **Beads:** Magic Scraps; **Printed twist tie:** Pebbles Inc.; **Silver clip:** Scrapworks; **Letter stamps:** PSX Design; **Label maker:**
Dymo; **Computer fonts:** 2Peas Weathered Fence, 2Peas Fancy Free, 2Peas Renaissance and 2Peas Task List, downloaded from
www.twopeasinabucket.com.

...the memory of love will bring you *home*

The Memory of Love

SUPPLIES   *Pages by Mellette Berezoski*
Patterned papers: Anna Griffin and K & Company; **Letter rub-ons, printed tag, brads and ribbon:** Making Memories; **Letter stickers:** Sonnets, Creative Imaginations; **Bookplate:** Magic Scraps; **Postal sticker and letter charms:** K & Company; **Antique clip:** EK Success; **Clock hands:** Walnut Hollow; **Photo turn:** 7gypsies; **Jewelry tags:** Two Peas in a Bucket; **Computer font:** GF Halda, downloaded from the Internet.

mellette's manner

1. **SEWING AND STITCHING.** A trusty old sewing machine lends a very hands-on feel to Mellette's pages, giving a sense of softness and stability at the same time.

2. **PATTERNED PAPERS.** Mellette has a special gift for combining just the right patterned papers that work perfectly with her overall layout. Her foundations are created with patterned papers, and she often includes additional patterned-paper accents. "Patterned papers take up most of my scrap room," says Mellette. "I'm hopelessly addicted." Mellette often creates pages that combine stripes and florals in wonderful harmony.

3. **FLORALS.** Sometimes soft and delicate, other times bold and bright, floral designs are a hallmark of Mellette's layouts.

4. **LITTLE DETAILS.** Mellette has a tremendous talent for bringing together myriad embellishments that communicate her vision beautifully. You get the sense that each one is chosen with love, with intention.

5. **ONE LARGE FOCAL-POINT PHOTO COMPLEMENTED BY A FEW CONSIDERABLY SMALLER ONES.** Building her layouts around a focal-point photo (think charm) is another characteristic of Mellette's creative manner. From there she adds additional photos that support the main photo, completing her vision.

Do You See What I See?

SUPPLIES   *Page by Joy Bohon*
Patterned paper: Paper House Productions; **Transparency:** 3M; **Rubber stamps:** Limited Edition Rubber Stamps and Fontwerks;
Stamping ink: StazOn, Tsukineko; Memories, Stewart Superior Corporation; **Photo turn:** 7gypsies; **Brads:** Lost Art Treasures;
Computer fonts: GF Ordner Inverted and Perpetua, downloaded from the Internet.

Documentation of a Friendship

SUPPLIES   *Pages by Joy Bohon*
Patterned paper: Karen Foster Design; **Transparency:** 3M; **Rubber stamps:** Limited Edition Rubber Stamps; **Stamping ink:** StazOn
and VersaMark, Tsukineko; Memories, Stewart Superior Corporation; **Embossing powder:** Stamp-n-Stuff, Stampendous!; **Epoxy letters:** Creative Imaginations; **Photo turns:** 7gypsies; **Brads:** Lost Art Treasures; **Computer fonts:** Dirty Ego, Casablanca Antique and
Eras Bold ITC, downloaded from the Internet; **Other:** Twill and flower.

joy's manner

1. **WORDS.** One of the hallmarks of Joy's pages is her free-flowing, intensive journaling style. Her pages are filled with words that directly communicate her vision.

2. **FOCUS ON FEELINGS RATHER THAN EVENTS.** In general, Joy's pages are not event oriented, but rather "speak of my feelings, my dreams, to say the things I truly feel as I consider my children, to pass the message on to them." What a wonderful gift she's giving to her daughters through her rich journaling manner.

3. **FUNKY FONTS.** Joy has developed a love for funky, unique fonts (both computer and stamps). She creates graphic, bold titles that wonderfully complement her photography.

4. **NUMBERS.** You'll often find a number or two within Joy's layouts. It's simply something she loves to incorporate into her design. They're often bold numerals that enhance the vision she's attempting to communicate.

5. **DRAMATIC COLOR CONTRASTS.** According to Joy, "I love dramatic contrasts in a page and how a white background with bold text accomplishes this look for me. I love to add small touches of red for vibrancy." You'll often see pages from Joy combining red, black and white. This allows her to focus on the photos and the story she's communicating through her journaling.

6. **CLOSE-UP PHOTOS.** Joy's photos are dynamic and full of her subjects' personalities. She has a knack for matching these photos to the stories she wants to tell.

The Power of Words

SUPPLIES *Pages by Carrie Colbert*
Patterned papers: KI Memories, Chatterbox and American Crafts; **Vellum:** American Crafts; **Leather flowers, photo corners and brad:** Making Memories; **Computer fonts:** Messy G ("The Power of") by Gillian Nelson and Mechanical Fun ("Words"), downloaded from the Internet.

Brighten My World

SUPPLIES *Page by Carrie Colbert*
Patterned paper and rub-ons: KI Memories; **Mailbox letters:** Making Memories; **Clay embellishment:** Li'l Davis Designs; **Computer fonts:** 2Peas Weathered Fence (journaling) and 2Peas Stop Sign (title), downloaded from *www.twopeasinabucket.com*.

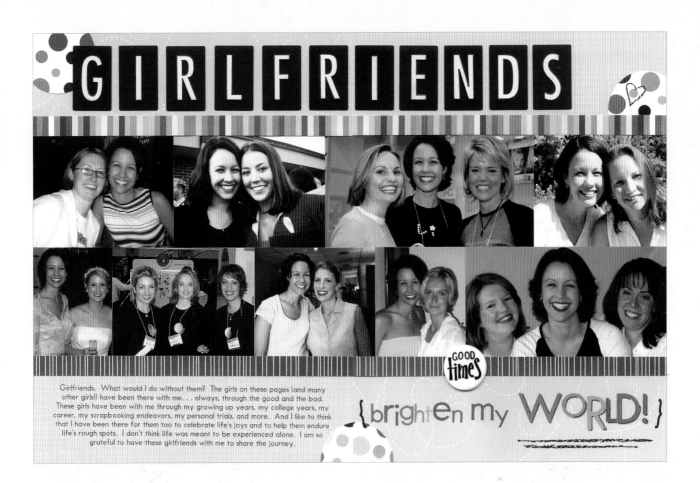

Girlfriends. What would I do without them? The girls on these pages (and many other girls!) have been there with me. . . always, through the good and the bad. These girls have been with me through my growing up years, my college years, my career, my scrapbooking endeavors, my personal trials, and more. And I like to think that I have been there for them too to celebrate life's joys and to help them endure life's rough spots. I don't think life was meant to be experienced alone. I am so grateful to have these girlfriends with me to share the journey.

GOOD times

{brighten my WORLD!}

carrie's manner

1. **HAPPINESS.** Carrie uses bright patterned papers to communicate a lightness of spirit and a sense of fun. They're simply uplifting to view. Bold titles also complement and add to this positive overall feeling.

2. **COLOR PHOTOS.** Using a variety of color photos is one of the hallmarks of Carrie's manner.

3. **AN ENGINEER'S EYE.** Carrie combines her professional life and her creative life into her scrapbooking. She precisely sketches out each design on graph paper before beginning the process of putting it all together.

4. **LINES AND STRIPES.** Carrie's love of stripes and straight lines is evident on almost every layout she creates. She's very adept at using lines to assist in the flow of each page.

5. **HEARTFELT, INTROSPECTIVE JOURNALING.** Carrie says, "I love using my scrapbooks as a place to document my personal growth." Carrie stretches herself and takes

advantage of the opportunity to reflect upon and even grow through the creative process of scrapbooking.

6. **A SENTIMENT OF GRATITUDE.** Carrie also tends to focus her pages on the things she's thankful for in her life. In line with her introspective journaling, this is what she really wants to communicate in her scrapbooks.

7. **FLOW.** Carrie is great at establishing flow within her layouts by strategically placing embellishments to guide the eye through the design.

8. **PICTURES OF CARRIE.** Carrie is a scrapbooker without children (yet!), so the heart of her pages feature photos of her. Her pages focus on her story—the things happening in her life now and in her own history.

identify your style

Maybe you're wondering to yourself, "What is my style?" I actually believe you already know all about it—it's a part of you deep down in your core self. It influences so many things you do and the choices you make in your life—how you decorate, how you plan your day, how you dress. Sometimes it helps to have someone give you a few prompts to bring an awareness of your manner to the surface.

So, right now, go and get your scrapbook albums and choose six of your favorite pages. Slip the pages out of your album and place them on a table in front of you.

1. Go through each page and make a list of the products you've used to design each page (Patterned paper? Metal embellishments? Alphabet stickers? Computer-generated journaling? A particular brand of cardstock?).

2. Look at each page and make a note of any special techniques you've used on the page (heat embossing? Paper tearing? Acrylic painting? Color blocking?).

3. Make a list about what you love about each page (is it the journaling? The photographs? The design?).

4. Make a list of the notes you've made about each page. What products and techniques do you seem to use over and over again? What "speaks" to you about YOUR pages? I bet you're much closer to answering the question, "what's my style?"

5. If you're still having problems identifying your style, hand your pages to a good scrapbooking friend and ask her to answer the questions that I've listed above. She may be able to help you "see" your style.

create a style file

One way to go about continuing to define your creative manner is to develop a style file—a book (or literally a file) that's simply all about things that visually appeal to you. Go through magazines and cut out photos, images, colors, typefaces, etc. that speak to you in one way or another. Gather bits of paper, notes from friends and scraps of patterned paper and line them up or collage them together—just get them down on paper.

When you begin creating your style file, you don't need to figure out or analyze why something appeals to you. Don't be critical or judgmental of any of your choices. Know that somewhere inside of you there's a reason for your attraction to a particular element or image. As your style file grows, you'll begin to see patterns that reveal things about your particular creative manner. Maybe you love the look of bold typefaces, or black-and-white designs, or bursts of strong color here and there. The idea is to take these little creative inspirations and use them to your advantage on your journey to embracing your personal style and scrapbooking meaningful pages.

We live in the age of information. Luckily for us this means it's also the age of inspiration—it's everywhere! Magazines showcase the latest and greatest design and product ideas. Online scrapbook galleries are available for instant inspiration at all hours of the day. I love seeing all the fantastic, creative things people are doing in our hobby. Learn from others. Be inspired by others. Take advantage of this chance to define your own manner by spending some time looking at others' pages and listing your likes and dislikes. And remember, scrapbooking is not a competition. It's the personal expression and record of your memories. Embrace your own manner and take your own scrapbooking to the next level.

My style file is filled with images that are inspiring and interesting to me. I write notes in my book, add pages from magazines, scraps of scrapbook paper, embellishments, random pieces of stuff, etc. Sometimes it's organized, and sometimes it's messy. My notes are generally reflective thoughts about what I found to be cool about each image—what made me want to keep it in the first place. In attempting to define why I'm attracted to something, I learn more about the things I love—more about my personal manner. Sometimes I get ideas for embellishments or page themes from my style file, but for the most part it's simply a creative exercise. A way to stretch my designing muscles. A chance to play. A chance to reflect on things I find visually stimulating. A style file is really a chance to explore what you love, helping you gain confidence in your manner.

SUPPLIES *Page by Ali Edwards*
Patterned papers: Chatterbox, KI Memories, 7gypsies, Mustard Moon and K & Company; **Embossed vellum:** K & Company; **Circle accents:** Nostalgiques, EK Success; **"Mine" accent:** KI Memories; **Punch:** Marvy Uchida; **Ribbon:** May Arts; **Square letters:** Li'l Davis Designs; **Foam stamps, acrylic paint and rub-ons:** Making Memories; **Other:** Manila folder.

make your style unique

Now that you've started to identify your style, I suggest that you find a way to make it unique. Stop for a minute and think about what's unique to you. Is there a symbol (a rose, a tiara, a zebra) that defines who you are? What about one word that describes you? Do you have a favorite color or a special nickname? Take whatever it is that makes you unique and turn it into your personal mark, a logo, per se. Add it to each page you create!

One of the things I've always loved and collected is the letter "A." And I fully admit that I love alphabet embellishments: stickers, stamps, accents— you name it, and I probably have it! When I began scrapbooking, I started using the letter "S" as a special mark on each of Simon's pages. It was a simple way to utilize all those cool embellishments. Now, coming up with different graphic concoctions using initials on my layouts is something I challenge myself to do on just about every page. Sometimes it's simply a letter stamp, while in other designs it's a complicated creation using the computer or a compilation of other elements. Finding something you love and translating it into a "mark" for yourself is a great way to make your pages truly unique. Just think about how much your future generations will enjoy the treasure hunt of finding your mark on each page!

Chapter Checklist

5 WAYS TO IDENTIFY YOUR OWN STYLE

1. *Identify why your favorite layouts are your favorites.*

2. *Make a list of your favorite techniques or products—that you actually use!*

3. *Create your own style file.*

4. *Ask a scrapbooking friend to define your style.*

5. *Incorporate a "symbol" of you on every page.*

the greatest gifts

I believe that scrapbooks are one of the greatest gifts we can give to our families and to ourselves. They represent our memories recorded and brought to life again on pieces of paper. Moments preserved. Our history. Our feelings and hopes and fears and lessons learned. A chance for reflection. For looking back, addressing the present, and looking to the future. What a very cool hobby this is indeed.

Create

SUPPLIES   *Page by Ali Edwards*
Patterned paper: Rusty Pickle; **Textured cardstock:** Bazzill Basics Paper; **Vellum:** Autumn Leaves; **Photo corners:** Nostalgiques, EK Success; **Photo turns:** 7gypsies; **Brads:** twopeasinabucket.com; **"Live Your Passion" sticker:** Wordsworth; **Letter stamps:** PSX Design and Ma Vinci's Reliquary; **Stamping ink:** Ranger Industries and Hero Arts.